First World War
and Army of Occupation
War Diary
France, Belgium and Germany

20 DIVISION
Divisional Troops
Royal Army Veterinary Corps
32 Mobile Veterinary Section
23 July 1915 - 28 March 1919

WO95/2110/3

The Naval & Military Press Ltd
www.nmarchive.com
Published in association with The National Archives

Published by

The Naval & Military Press Ltd

Unit 10 Ridgewood Industrial Park,

Uckfield, East Sussex,

TN22 5QE England

Tel: +44 (0) 1825 749494

www.naval-military-press.com

www.nmarchive.com

This diary has been reprinted in facsimile from the original. Any imperfections are inevitably reproduced and the quality may fall short of modern type and cartographic standards.

Contents

Document type	Place/Title	Date From	Date To
Heading	2110/3		
Heading	20th Division 32nd Mobile Vety Section Jly 1915-Mar 1919		
Heading	20th Division 32nd Mob. Vet. Sect. Vol I Jly to Oct 15		
War Diary	Larkhill	23/07/1915	23/07/1915
War Diary	Harne	24/07/1915	25/07/1915
War Diary	Wizernes	26/07/1915	26/07/1915
War Diary	Lumbres	27/07/1915	28/07/1915
War Diary	Lynde	28/07/1915	29/07/1915
War Diary	Merris	30/07/1915	27/08/1915
War Diary	Estaires	28/08/1915	07/10/1915
Heading	20th Division 32nd Mob. Vet. Sect. Vol. 2 Oct 15		
War Diary	Estaires	08/10/1915	27/10/1915
Heading	20th Division 32nd Mob. Vet. Sect. Vol. 3 Nov. 15		
War Diary	Estaires	28/10/1915	30/11/1915
Heading	20th Division 32nd Mob. Vet. Sect. Vol. 4		
War Diary	Estaires	01/12/1915	31/12/1915
Heading	32nd Mob. Vet. Sect. Vol. 5		
War Diary	Oxelaere	23/01/1916	31/01/1916
War Diary	Estaires	14/01/1916	14/01/1916
War Diary	Stenbecque	15/01/1916	22/01/1916
War Diary	Estaires	01/01/1916	13/01/1916
Heading	32nd Mob. Vet. Sect. Vol. 6		
War Diary	Arneke	01/02/1916	04/02/1916
War Diary	Ledringham	05/02/1916	14/02/1916
War Diary	Watou	15/02/1916	29/02/1916
Heading	32 MVS Vol 7		
War Diary	Watou	01/03/1916	30/04/1916
War Diary	Ledingham	01/05/1916	21/05/1916
War Diary	Hamhock	23/05/1916	17/07/1916
War Diary	Ladingham	18/07/1916	31/07/1916
War Diary	St Leger Les Authie	01/08/1916	17/08/1916
War Diary	Hulem	18/08/1916	18/08/1916
War Diary	Macfer	19/08/1916	19/08/1916
War Diary	Havernas	20/08/1916	20/08/1916
War Diary	Dowar	21/08/1916	21/08/1916
War Diary	Treue	22/08/1916	22/08/1916
War Diary	Meaulte	23/08/1916	06/09/1916
War Diary	Corbie	07/09/1916	10/09/1916
War Diary	Meaulte	11/09/1916	30/09/1916
Heading	32nd Mobile. Vet. Section. 20 Div October 1916 Vol 14		
War Diary	Meaulte	01/10/1916	15/10/1916
War Diary	Corbie	16/10/1916	31/10/1916
War Diary	Belloy-Sur-Somme	01/11/1916	14/11/1916
War Diary	Ailly	15/11/1916	15/11/1916
War Diary	Corbie	16/11/1916	11/12/1916
War Diary	Carnoy	12/12/1916	24/12/1916
War Diary	Corbie	25/12/1916	31/12/1916
Miscellaneous	32 Mobile Veterinary Section. A.V.C.		

Miscellaneous	Establishment of Animals 31.12.16 as per D.D. Remounts 4th Army No 4/3/1 20 Division No. Q/20/4141/36		
Heading	War Diary of the 32nd Mobile Vet. Section January 1917 Vol 17		
War Diary	Corbie	01/01/1917	04/01/1917
War Diary	Carnoy	05/01/1917	31/01/1917
Heading	War Diary of 32nd Mob. Vet. Section 20th Division February 1917 Vol 18		
War Diary	Heilly	02/02/1917	07/02/1917
War Diary	Carnoy	09/02/1917	27/02/1917
Heading	War Diary of 32nd Mobile Veterinary Section March 1917 Vol 19		
War Diary	Carnoy	02/03/1917	20/03/1917
War Diary	Briqueterie	21/03/1917	31/03/1917
Heading	War Diary of 32nd Mobile Veterinary Section April 1917 Vol 20		
War Diary	Briqueterie	02/04/1917	03/04/1917
War Diary	Le Transloy	04/04/1917	27/04/1917
War Diary	Rocquigny	28/04/1917	30/04/1917
Heading	War Diary May 1917 32nd Mobile Veterinary Section Vol 21		
War Diary	Rocquigny	01/05/1917	23/05/1917
War Diary	Bapaume	23/05/1917	31/05/1917
Heading	War Diary of 32nd Mobile Vety Sect June 1917 Vol 22		
War Diary		01/06/1917	30/06/1917
Heading	War Diary 32 MV Section July 1917 Vol 23		
War Diary	Bernaville	02/07/1917	21/07/1917
War Diary	Proven	22/07/1917	31/07/1917
War Diary	Proven E 18.b.11 Sheet 27	01/08/1917	06/08/1917
War Diary	A.9.c.73. Sheet 28	06/08/1917	31/08/1917
Heading	War Diary 32nd Mobile Vet. Section Sept. 1917 Vol 25		
War Diary	E.18.b.11 Sheet 27	01/09/1917	11/09/1917
War Diary	A.9.c.7.3 Sheet 28	11/09/1917	30/09/1917
War Diary		01/10/1917	15/10/1917
War Diary	Moislains	16/10/1917	22/11/1917
War Diary	Couzeacourt	23/11/1917	30/11/1917
War Diary	Moislains	01/12/1917	04/12/1917
War Diary	Meaulte	05/12/1917	05/12/1917
War Diary	Amplier	06/12/1917	06/12/1917
War Diary	Petit Fillieres	07/12/1917	07/12/1917
War Diary	Marconnelle	08/12/1917	08/12/1917
War Diary	Racquinghem	12/12/1917	04/01/1918
War Diary	Meteren	06/01/1918	06/01/1918
War Diary	Westoutre	07/01/1918	15/02/1918
War Diary	Pradelles	16/02/1918	16/02/1918
War Diary	Racquinghem	17/02/1918	23/02/1918
War Diary	Ercheux	24/02/1918	28/02/1918
War Diary	Ercheu	05/03/1918	31/03/1918
War Diary	Sains En Amienois	01/04/1918	15/04/1918
War Diary	Buigny	16/04/1918	30/04/1918
War Diary	Mingoval	01/05/1918	23/05/1918
War Diary	Petit Servins	24/05/1918	05/10/1918
War Diary	Mingoval	06/10/1918	31/10/1918
War Diary	Velu	01/11/1918	01/11/1918
War Diary	Cambrai	02/11/1918	03/11/1918

War Diary	Rieux	04/11/1918	06/11/1918
War Diary	Vadegies	07/11/1918	08/11/1918
War Diary	Wargnies Le Grand	09/11/1918	09/11/1918
War Diary	Bavay	10/11/1918	23/11/1918
War Diary	Jelain	24/11/1918	25/11/1918
War Diary	Vendigies	26/11/1918	26/11/1918
War Diary	Rieux	27/11/1918	28/11/1918
War Diary	Cambrai	29/11/1918	29/11/1918
War Diary	Beugnatre	30/11/1918	30/11/1918
War Diary	Bienvillers	01/12/1918	01/12/1918
War Diary	Pas.	03/12/1918	01/01/1919
War Diary	Grincourt	02/01/1919	31/01/1919
Miscellaneous	20th Div.		
War Diary	Grincourt	01/02/1919	28/03/1919

20TH DIVISION

32ND MOBILE VETY SECTION

JLY 1915 - MAR 1919

20th Division

121/7595.

32nd Mob: Vet: Sect:

Vol. I

July to Oct 15

Jy 15
Mar 19

AWD

Instructions regarding War Diaries and Intelligence Summaries are contained in F. S. Regs., Part II. and the Staff Manual respectively. Title Pages will be prepared in manuscript.

No 32 MOBILE VETERINARY SECTION No. Date 20th DIVISION

WAR DIARY
or
INTELLIGENCE SUMMARY
(Erase heading not required.)

I

Army Form C. 2118.

No 32 MOBILE VETERINARY SECTION No. Date 20th DIVISION

Place	Date	Hour	Summary of Events and Information	Remarks and references to Appendices
Larkhill	23.7.15	1-15 p.m.	No 32 Mobile Veterinary Section, 20th Division, left AMESBURY station with Capt. T. Lishman, A.V.C., commanding. Strength 26, including 2 A.S.C. drivers attached, and 20 riding horses, 4 light draught mules, and 2 limbered G.S. wagons.	
	"	2-45 "	Arrived Southampton.	
	"	3-15 "	Embarked on S.S. African Prince.	
		5-0 "	Sailed	
Havre	24.7.15	3-15 a.m.	Arrived and lay outside the harbour.	
"	"	7 "	Disembarked, off saddled, and remained on docks, where men and horses were fed.	
"	"			
"	"	2-30 p.m.	Marched to No 5 Rest Camp. Received order to entrain at Gare des Marchandises the following morning at 8-30 a.m.	
"	25 "	8-30 a.m.	Entrained	
"	"	12 noon	The train left the station. One case of colic in a horse of 93rd R.F.A.	
WIZERNES	26"	8-20 a.m.	Arrived and disentrained. Received orders to proceed to Lumbres by road, which lies 6 miles S.W. of St Omer.	
		11 p.m.	Arrived, and went into billets. The men going into a barn at the Brasserie, M. Mayeux, and the horses into a field adjoining.	
LUMBRE	27"		Remained in billets. Took into Hospital Genl. Davie's charger and a horse and mule from Divisional Sigs. (cable section).	

1875 Wt. W593/826 1,000,000 4/15 J.B.C. & A. A.D.S.S./Forms/C. 2118.

Army Form C. 2[illegible]

Instructions regarding War Diaries and Intelligence Summaries are contained in F. S. Regs., Part II. and the Staff Manual respectively. Title Pages will be prepared in manuscript.

WAR DIARY
or
INTELLIGENCE SUMMARY
(Erase heading not required.)

2

Place	Date	Hour	Summary of Events and Information	Remarks and references to Appendices
LUMBRES	28 7/15	7-30 a.m.	Left Lumbres and marched to LYNDE, a distance of 13 miles	
LYNDE	"	2 p.m.	arrived at LYnde and went into Billets. Treated one case of Div. Signals, picked up nail.	
"	29 7/15	6-30 a.m.	Left LYNDE and marched to Merris (MERRIS) via Hazebrouck and Borre, arriving in billets at 12 midday. No casualties were encountered during the march	
MERRIS	30 7/15		Remained in billets the whole day. Received into Hospital for treatment 5 horses from various units of the Division	
"	31 7/15		Remaining in Billets. Received for evacuation 1 horse, & for treatment 4. Took over Vety. charge of Headquarter units of the Division.	
"	1 8/15		Remaining in Billets. Received another six horses and mules for treatment.	
"	2 8/15		Remaining in Billets. Received for treatment 1 horse & 1 mule from 83rd Field Coy. R.E.	
"	3 8/15		Remaining in billets. Horse of 83rd Fld. Coy R.E. died from septic pneumonia.	
"	4 8/15		Remaining in billets. The men of the Section employed in dressing cases & burying the horse of the R.E.	

1875 Wt. W593/826 1,000,000 4/15 J.B.C. & A. A.D.S.S./Forms/C. 2118.

Instructions regarding War Diaries and Intelligence Summaries are contained in F. S. Regs., Part II. and the Staff Manual respectively. Title Pages will be prepared in manuscript.

WAR DIARY
or
INTELLIGENCE SUMMARY
(Erase heading not required.)

3

Army Form C. 2

Place	Date	Hour	Summary of Events and Information	Remarks and references to Appendices
Merris	5.8/15		Dressing cases sent for treatment in Hospital Lines. Selected 20 animals for evacuation on the following day.	
"	6 8/15		The twenty horses for evacuation, made up of 16 surgical cases, 1 medical, 2 specific, and 1 mare in foal, left the hospital at 8 a.m. for the railhead at LA GORGUE, a distance of 10 Kilometres. They were entrained at 2 p.m. and sent to No 5 Veterinary Hospital, Abbeville; the party of 3 men being in charge of Act. Cpl. Pollexfen, A.V.C., who took with him copies of indents for No 1 Advanced Depot of Veterinary Stores, Abbeville from where he was instructed to fetch the stores to the railhead, and then up to the refilling point on the supply lorries.	
"	7 8/15		Sent in to A.D.V.S. a return showing that 37 horses had been treated in the Section during the week ending Thursday the 5.8.15	
"	8 8/15		Corporal Pollexfen and three men of the conducting party returned to the Section having handed over the sick horses and returned with Veterinary Stores for the Vety. Officers of the Division.	

Instructions regarding War Diaries and Intelligence Summaries are contained in F. S. Regs., Part II. and the Staff Manual respectively. Title Pages will be prepared in manuscript.

WAR DIARY
or
INTELLIGENCE SUMMARY
(Erase heading not required.)

4

Army Form C. [illegible]18

Place	Date	Hour	Summary of Events and Information	Remarks and references to Appendices
MERRIS	9 8/15		Received several more horses into the Section for treatment.	
"	"	12-30 p.m.	Medical inspection of men of the Section by Medical Officer i/c of Brigade area. No 6753 Pte H. Phillips was sent to Hospital.	
"	10 8/15		Acting Corporal No 8035 R.D.J. Pollexfen A.V.C. was returned to the ranks for inefficiency, & No 6535 Pte G. Yeo. A.V.C. was promoted to Act. Corporal.	
"	11 8/15		The flies were found very troublesome, and in the cases of wounds that could not be bandaged, an efficacious dressing was found in Acid Borici 3 parts & Pulv. Sulphur 1 part.	
"	12 8/15		Remaining in billets receiving cases for admission and dressing out-patients.	
"	13 8/15		Despatched with 1 Corporal & 4 men to No 5 Vety. Hospital, Abbeville, 26 sick horses one of which was a case suspected of mange. One mule died in the Section (from 83rd Field Coy. R.E.) suffering from oedema and subcutaneous emphysema.	
"	14 8/15		Sent in to A.D.V.S. a return showing that 45 horses had been admitted to the Section for treatment during the week ending 12.8.15	

1875 Wt. W593/826 1,000,000 4/15 J.B.C. & A. A.D.S.S./Forms/C. 2118.

Instructions regarding War Diaries and Intelligence Summaries are contained in F. S. Regs., Part II. and the Staff Manual respectively. Title Pages will be prepared in manuscript.

WAR DIARY
or
INTELLIGENCE SUMMARY
(Erase heading not required.)

Army Form C. 2[illegible]

5

Place	Date	Hour	Summary of Events and Information	Remarks and references to Appendices
MERRIS	15 8/15		Admitted for diagnosis and treatment horse No 23 of 92nd Bde R.F.A. with ulcerative lymphangitis. Examined pus at No 4 Mobile Laboratory of the 2nd Army for the Cryptococcus of Rivolta with negative results, and obtained a negative result with the mallein test. Conducting party under Corpl. Mold returned with Stores from Abbeville.	
"	16 8/15		Nothing to report. The Sectioned occupied in dressing cases — both in patients and out.	
"	17 8/15		Borrowed a float from a Villager to fetch in two horses that had been badly kicked in the lines of the 91st Bde R.F.A.	
"	18 8/15		Nothing to report. Received a wire giving information of two horses left behind by 59th Infty. Bde.	
"	19 8/15		Collected the horses mentioned in yesterdays wire. One from DOULIEU, I 4 Map 5A. left by 11th K.R.R.; and one from OUTERSTEÈNE, near Doulieu.	
"	20 8/15		Sent in A.F.A 2000 to A.D.V.S. showing that 68 animals had been	

1875 Wt. W593/826 1,000,000 4/15 J.B.C. & A. A.D.S.S./Forms/C. 2118.

Instructions regarding War Diaries and Intelligence Summaries are contained in F. S. Regs., Part II. and the Staff Manual respectively. Title Pages will be prepared in manuscript.

WAR DIARY
or
INTELLIGENCE SUMMARY
(Erase heading not required.)

Army Form C. 21

6

Place	Date	Hour	Summary of Events and Information	Remarks and references to Appendices
			under treatment in the Section during the previous week, and of these 6 were cured & returned to their units, 26 were sent to No 5 Vety. Hospital, Abbeville on 13·8·15, and 36 were remaining either under treatment for return to their units or else too lame to be walked to the rail head. Sent to Abbeville 12 more sick animals.	
MERRIS	21 8/15		Hospital work with 24 cases in the section Lines. Received for treatment or evacuation 5 more cases.	
"	22 8/15		Corporal Mold and one man forming the conducting party that left on 20·8·15 returned bringing stores & microscope for A.D.V.S. Received into section 13 mules from 20th Div. Amm. Col. and 1 horse from D 93rd R.F.A., No 6454 Pte H. GASTON sent to Hospital.	
"	23 8/15		Despatched from the railhead, at LA GORGUE, 8 horses and 14 mules, under charge of Cpl Mold and two men. No 1734 Pte. A. Newman went sick to 60th Field Ambulance.	
"	24 8/15		Remained in billets dressing cases.	
"	25 8/15		The section was inspected by the D.D.V.S.	
"	26 8/15		Five incurable cases were destroyed	
"	27 8/15		Nineteen horses and three mules sent to ABBEVILLE with Cpl. Yeo & 2 men. 83 animals were treated during the week ending 26·8·15 of which 20 horses and 14 mules were evacuated to ABBEVILLE.	

Instructions regarding War Diaries and Intelligence Summaries are contained in F. S. Regs., Part II. and the Staff Manual respectively. Title Pages will be prepared in manuscript.

WAR DIARY
or
INTELLIGENCE SUMMARY
(Erase heading not required.)

Army Form C. 2118

7

Place	Date	Hour	Summary of Events and Information	Remarks and references to Appendices
ESTAIRES	28/8/15	8 a.m.	Left MERRIS and marched to ESTAIRES.	
"	"	10 "	Arrived ESTAIRES and proceeded to billet in NOVEOU MONDE. Billet dirty and very unsatisfactory. Two cases admitted.	
"	29/8/15	—	Proceed to take up new billet on ESTAIRES-NEUF BERQUIN Road ¼ mile north of A in ESTAIRES map 5A HAZEBROUCK. Admitted 7 cases.	
"	30/8/15	—	Admitted 5 cases. Sent to ABBEVILLE, No 5 Vety. Hospital 10 horses and 2 mules with Serjt. Miller & 1 man, for treatment or evacuation.	
"	31/8/15	—	Admitted 6 cases. Most of the day spent in cleaning the billet & erecting horse lines.	
"	1/9/15	—	Eight horses and 3 mules despatched to ABBEVILLE in charge of Cpl. Mold and 1 man.	
"	2/9/15	—	Received into the Section 3 horses and 2 mules. Procured ashes in NOVEAU MONDE for laying a track from the road to the horse standings. 71 horses had been admitted during the last week.	
"	3/9/15	—	No cases admitted, most of the day spent in cleaning the billet and laying ash tracks up to the standings.	
"	4/9/15	—	Two cases admitted. Repairing of billet continued.	
"	5/9/15	—	Six cases admitted. " " "	

1875 Wt. W593/826 1,000,000 4/15 J.B.C. & A. A.D.S.S./Forms/C. 2118.

Instructions regarding War Diaries and Intelligence Summaries are contained in F. S. Regs., Part II. and the Staff Manual respectively. Title Pages will be prepared in manuscript.

WAR DIARY
or
INTELLIGENCE SUMMARY
(Erase heading not required.)

8

Army Form C. 2

Place	Date	Hour	Summary of Events and Information	Remarks and references to Appendices
ESTAIRES	6/9/15	—	Five cases admitted. Cpl Yeo, and 1 man took 9 horses and 5 mules to ABBEVILLE.	
"	7/9/15	—	Two cases admitted. No 6933 Pte Sadler, A.V.C. joined from No 3 Veterinary Hospital in place of 6547 Pte H. Booth who left sick on 17th August.	
"	8/9/15	—	Eleven horses admitted to the section.	
"	9/9/15	—	Fifteen horses & mules admitted.	
"	10/9/15	—	Twenty nine animals evacuated to the L. of C. Seven more animals admitted.	
"	11/9/15	—	Nine animals evacuated to the L. of C.	
"	12/9/15	—	Three horses admitted. No 472 Sergt Stafford, A.V.C. joined the section from No 3 Mob. Vety. Sect.	
"	13/9/15	—	Seven horses admitted.	
"	14/9/15	—	Three horses admitted. Eight transferred sick to No 5 Veterinary Hospital ABBEVILLE.	
"	15/9/15	—	Three cases admitted.	
"	16"	—	One case admitted. Conducting party returned with medicines.	
"	17"	—	Two cases admitted.	

Army Form C. 2118

9

WAR DIARY
or
INTELLIGENCE SUMMARY
(Erase heading not required.)

Instructions regarding War Diaries and Intelligence Summaries are contained in F. S. Regs., Part II. and the Staff Manual respectively. Title Pages will be prepared in manuscript.

Place	Date	Hour	Summary of Events and Information	Remarks and references to Appendices
ESTAIRES	18 9/15	—	15 cases admitted twelve of which were from the Guards Division. 4 cases required the hire of a float.	
"	19 "	—	24 sick animals transferred to L. of C. under Corpl. A. Mold. 1 case admitted.	
"	20 "	—	No 7459 L/Cpl. W. E. McGuinness & No 8681 L/Cpl. A. J. Freezer both of A.V.C. joined the Section from 60th Infty. Bde, & 61st Ifty. Bde. respectively after being relieved by Serjts. of the A.V.C. 2 cases admitted.	
"	21 "	—	Conducting party returned with Vety. medicines. 9 cases were admitted	
"	22 "	—	15 horses transferred to L. of C. under charge of Serjt. Stafford. No 6933 Pte J. Sadler, A.V.C. admitted to Hospital. 8 cases admitted to section.	
"	23 "	—	Opened an advanced dressing post at NOVEAU MONDE, 1 Kilometre east of ESTAIRES. 7 cases admitted to the Section.	
"	24 "	—	10 cases admitted and 20 animals transferred sick to ABBEVILLE. Conducting party that left on 22nd returned.	
"	25 "	—	14 cases admitted and 10 transferred sick to ABBEVILLE.	
"	26 "	—	3 cases admitted. Conducting party that left on 24th returned short of 1 man – No 8035 Pte Pollexfen having been left at Hospital at ABBEVILLE. Brought 1 case in a float from advanced dressing post.	

1875 Wt. W593/826 1,000,000 4/15 J.B.C. & A. A.D.S.S./Forms/C. 2118.

Instructions regarding War Diaries and Intelligence Summaries are contained in F. S. Regs., Part II. and the Staff Manual respectively. Title Pages will be prepared in manuscript.

WAR DIARY
or
INTELLIGENCE SUMMARY
(Erase heading not required.)

Army Form C. 21[illegible]

10

Place	Date	Hour	Summary of Events and Information	Remarks and references to Appendices
ESTAIRES	27 9/15	—	Three cases admitted. Conducting party returned.	
"	28 9/15	—	Five cases admitted. 14 cases transferred to L. of C. under L/Cpl McGuinness & 1 man. [illegible] No 2919 Sergt H.E. WATKINS A.V.C. joined the Section from 92nd Bde. R.F.A.	
"	29 "	—	Nine cases admitted, one a case of tetanus from 20th Div. H.Q.	
"	30 "	—	Four cases admitted. No 80 Pte. H.G. GIBBS, A.V.C. reported his arrival from No 3 Veterinary Hospital for duty. Conducting party returned. Veterinary Stores received.	
"	1 10/15	—	Mule admitted with Tetanus from 20th Div. H.Q. died. 10 horses & 4 mules evacuated to Abbeville. 4 cases admitted.	
"	2 10/15	—	5 cases admitted.	
"	3 10/15	—	7 cases admitted. Conducting party returned; 5 horses and 3 mules evacuated to L of C.	
"	4 10/15	—	8 cases admitted. 1 destroyed suffering from open joint.	
"	5 "	—	4 cases admitted. 14 cases evacuated to Abbeville — 9 horses & 5 mules. Buried the horse destroyed yesterday. Conducting party returned.	
"	6 "	—	5 cases admitted;	
"	7 "	—	14 cases admitted; 12 horses & 4 mules evacuated; Conducting party returned.	

1875 Wt. W593/826 1,000,000 4/15 J.B.C. & A. A.D.S.S./Forms/C. 2118.

30th Division

32nd Mdn. Vet. Sects.
Vol. 2

121
7795.

Oct 15

[illegible]

Instructions regarding War Diaries and Intelligence Summaries are contained in F. S. Regs., Part II. and the Staff Manual respectively. Title Pages will be prepared in manuscript.

WAR DIARY
or
INTELLIGENCE SUMMARY
(Erase heading not required.)

Army Form C. 2118

Place	Date	Hour	Summary of Events and Information	Remarks and references to Appendices
ESTAIRES	8/10/15	—	Collected 1 horse of 454th Coy, A.S.C. from M. EMILE MOUQUET, LA COURONNE, near Vieux Berquin. 17 animals admitted to the Section	
"	9/10/15	—	4 cases admitted; 18 horses & 6 mules evacuated to L. of C. Conducting party returned	
"	10/10/15	—	9 cases admitted. Two Sergts. attached, awaiting instructions, went on 6 days leave to England.	
"	11 "	—	13 cases admitted & 13 transferred sick to L. of C. Conducting party returned.	
"	12 "	—	12 cases admitted. No T/1/38712 Dr W. MIZEN, A.S.C. produced a Drs note certifying the dangerous illness of his child, and was granted 6 days special leave by the G.O.C. Division.	
"	13 "	—	14 cases admitted. 18 horses & 6 mules transferred sick. Conducting party returned.	
"	14 "	—	Great difficulty was experienced in providing halters for sick horses evacuated to the L. of C. The Section had 100 hemp halters as part of its equipment, and when horses were taken to No 5 Veterinary Hospital, Abbeville either these halters were returned or the same number sent back to me in place of them. Suddenly this Veterinary Hospital stopped the return of halters with the result	

Instructions regarding War Diaries and Intelligence Summaries are contained in F. S. Regs., Part II. and the Staff Manual respectively. Title Pages will be prepared in manuscript.

Army Form C. 2118

WAR DIARY
or
INTELLIGENCE SUMMARY
(Erase heading not required.)

Place	Date	Hour	Summary of Events and Information	Remarks and references to Appendices
ESTAIRES	14/10/15	—	that after this had been done four times there were no halters left. I complained to the O.C., No 5 Veterinary Hospital about the matter, & he replied that all horses sent up country took with them serviceable head collars, and that when they were sent down sick their head collars should be sent with them. As regards this reply, in this Division at least, his statement that Remounts arrive with head collars is not accurate. The result was that head collars had to be kept in the Section when sick horses came in, & when they were transferred sick they accompanied them to the L. of C. Hospital. The headcollar being part of the bridle was part of the units equipment, & so finally units preferred to keep their sick sooner than part with their Regimental equipment with them. Another 100 hemp halters have arrived & it is hoped that they will be returned from Abbeville with the conducting parties so that the Section can return the head collars of the unit as soon as a sick horse is admitted. 7 cases admitted.	
"	15"	—	Conducting party returned; 13 horses transferred sick.	
"	16"	—	1 case admitted.	
"	17"	—	5 cases admitted. Conducting party returned	

Instructions regarding War Diaries and Intelligence Summaries are contained in F. S. Regs., Part II. and the Staff Manual respectively. Title Pages will be prepared in manuscript.

WAR DIARY
or
INTELLIGENCE SUMMARY
(Erase heading not required.)

Army Form C. 2118

Place	Date	Hour	Summary of Events and Information	Remarks and references to Appendices
ESTAIRES	17/10/15	—	Two Sergts returned from leave, & one was transferred to B Batty. 92nd Bde. R.F.A. & the other to the Div. Amm. Col. 15th Division	
"	18/10/15	—	9 cases admitted & 7 transferred sick. 1 case destroyed suffering from arthritis of pedal joint. Buried the carcase.	
"	19 "		Dr MIZEN, A.S.C. returned from leave. 7 cases admitted.	
"	20 "	—	8 cases admitted. 14 transferred sick. Sergt Watkins returned from leave, & transferred to 1st Army H.Q. at AIRE.	
"	21 "	—	Conducting party returned.	
"	22 "	—	2 cases admitted. Conducting party returned. Commenced mending out buildings to make winter stables.	
"	23 "	—	4 cases admitted. 6 cases transferred sick to L. of C. Making of stables continued.	
"	24 "	—	3 cases admitted. Making of stables continued.	
"	25 "	—	Two cases admitted. Stables finished, making accommodation for 40 animals. Horses put inside stables.	
"	26 "	—	2 cases admitted. 8 cases transferred sick. Hired float and brought in from LA MOTTE AU BOIS a horse of the 5th Drag. Gds.	
"	27 "	—	1 case admitted.	

20th Division

32nd Mob: Vet: Sect:
Vol: 3

L

121
7724

Nov. 15

[illegible]

[illegible]

Instructions regarding War Diaries and Intelligence Summaries are contained in F. S. Regs., Part II. and the Staff Manual respectively. Title Pages will be prepared in manuscript.

WAR DIARY
or
INTELLIGENCE SUMMARY
(Erase heading not required.)

Army Form C. 2118.

No. 32 MOBILE VETERINARY SECTION No. .... Date .... 20th DIVISION

Place	Date	Hour	Summary of Events and Information	Remarks and references to Appendices
ESTAIRES	28 10/15	—	3 cases admitted. Conducting party returned.	
"	29 "	—	5 cases admitted. No 1282 Pte GILBEY. J. from 'B' Batty 90th R.F.A.	
"	30 "	—	6 cases admitted. 13 cases transferred sick. Received from A.O.D. 50 horse rugs.	
"	31 "	—	2 cases admitted.	
"	1 11/15	—	3 cases admitted. 8 transferred sick. Conducting party returned. Received from A.O.D. 184 horse rugs.	
"	2 "	—	Applied to D.A.D.O.S. concerning the 210 horse rugs above the 24 the unit is entitled to & received a reply that a mistake had been made & that they would be called for. 5 cases admitted.	
"	3 "	—	7 cases admitted. 8 cases transferred sick. Conducting party returned.	
"	4 "	—	10 cases admitted. 7 cases transferred sick. Made arrangements in ESTAIRES for a daily supply of sawdust & shavings from a Military workshop.	
"	5 "	—	9 cases admitted. 8 cases transferred sick. Conducting party returned.	
"	6 "	—	14 cases admitted. 8 cases transferred sick.	
"	7 "	—	2 cases admitted. 16 cases transferred sick. Conducting party returned. The blankets of the section were disinfected at the divisional baths.	
"	8 "	—	13 cases admitted.	

1875 Wt. W593/826 1,000,000 4/15 J.B.C. & A. A.D.S.S./Forms/C. 2118.

Instructions regarding War Diaries and Intelligence Summaries are contained in F. S. Regs., Part II. and the Staff Manual respectively. Title Pages will be prepared in manuscript.

WAR DIARY
or
INTELLIGENCE SUMMARY
(Erase heading not required.)

Army Form C. 2118

No. 32 MOBILE VETERINARY SECTION No. .... Date .... 20th DIVISION

Place	Date	Hour	Summary of Events and Information	Remarks and references to Appendices
ESTAIRES	9.11.15	—	3 cases admitted. 16 transferred sick. Conducting party returned.	
"	10 "	—	16 cases admitted.	
"	11 "	—	6 cases admitted. 19 transferred sick. Conducting party returned. 6 loads of ashes obtained for putting on pathways to stables & the cook house.	
"	12 "	—	4 cases admitted.	
"	13 "	—	4 cases admitted. 8 transferred sick. Conducting party returned. 6 loads of ashes obtained for the billet.	
"	14 "	—	5 cases admitted.	
"	15 "	—	13 cases admitted. 18 transferred sick. Conducting party returned.	
"	16 "	—	17 cases admitted. 19 transferred sick.	
"	17 "	—	5 cases admitted. 13 cases transferred sick. Conducting party returned.	
"	18 "	—	6 cases admitted. 7 cases transferred sick. Conducting party returned.	
"	19 "	—	10 cases admitted. 11 transferred sick. Conducting party returned	
"	20 "	—	4 " " . 8 " " " " " & No. 283 Sergt. Anthony. E., No. 1535 Cpl Anderson. T. W., No. 5802 Pte Knowles. J., & No. 7483 Pte O'Donnell. J. all of A.V.C. arrived for duty having been transferred from No. 3 Veterinary Hospital, Boulogne.	

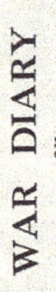

1875 Wt. W593/826 1,000,000 4/15 J.B.C. & A. A.D.S.S./Forms/C. 2118.

Instructions regarding War Diaries and Intelligence Summaries are contained in F. S. Regs., Part II. and the Staff Manual respectively. Title Pages will be prepared in manuscript.

WAR DIARY
or
INTELLIGENCE SUMMARY
(Erase heading not required.)

No. 32 MOBILE VETERINARY SECTION No. .... Date .... 20th DIVISION

Army Form C. 2118

Place	Date	Hour	Summary of Events and Information	Remarks and references to Appendices
ESTAIRES	21.11.15	—	49 cases admitted. 47 transferred sick. Conducting party returned.	
"	22"	—	6 cases admitted, 19 " " , " " ".	
"			No 261 Sergt A. Mold, No 8681 Cpl. Freezer. J.A., No 672 Private Barnes. A.J., & No 6510 Pte Rice. F.H. of the section transferred to No 3 Vety. Hospital, Boulogne. No 6723 Pte Chapman, H. was granted leave home from 22nd to 28th of the month.	
"	23"	—	17 cases admitted, 8 transferred sick, conducting party returned.	
"	24"	—	11 cases admitted, 24 transferred sick, conducting party returned, one of the cases admitted on 22nd with a septic leg had to be destroyed, & carcase was buried.	
"	25"	—	6 cases admitted, 6 transferred sick, conducting party returned.	
"	26"	—	3 cases admitted, conducting party returned.	
"	27"	—	4 cases admitted, conducting party returned.	
"	28"	—	20 cases admitted, 26 transferred sick.	
"	29"	—	1 case admitted. No 6723 Pte H. CHAPMAN, returned from leave having been delayed 1 day at Boulogne. No 6885 S.S. AUCHTERLONIE. J. arrived for duty from No 12 Vety. Hospital.	
"	30"	—	12 cases admitted. conducting party returned. 4 loads of ashes obtained for the billet. No 5636 S.S. Cpl A. LOGAN left for No 3 Vety. Hospital	

30.11.15 T. Lishman Capt. A.V.C.

1875 Wt. W593/826 1,000,000 4/15 J.B.C. & A. A.D.S.S./Forms/C. 2118.

20th Div

32nd Mdx: Vols: Sect:
Vol: 4

121
7935

Instructions regarding War Diaries and Intelligence Summaries are contained in F. S. Regs., Part II. and the Staff Manual respectively. Title Pages will be prepared in manuscript.

WAR DIARY
or
INTELLIGENCE SUMMARY
(Erase heading not required.)

No. 32 MOBILE VETERINARY SECTION
No. ....
Date ....
20th DIVISION

Army Form C. 2118

Place	Date	Hour	Summary of Events and Information	Remarks and references to Appendices
ESTAIRES	1 12/15	—	16 cases admitted, 12 cases transferred sick.	
"	2"	—	10 cases admitted, 16 cases transferred sick.	
"	3"	—	8 cases admitted, 9 cases transferred sick, Conducting party returned.	
"	4"	—	4 cases admitted, 4 cases transferred sick, Conducting party returned. 2 loads of cinders obtained for the billet.	
"	5"	—	8 cases admitted, 12 cases transferred sick, Blankets of the Section were disinfected & the men of the Section bathed at the Divisional baths.	
"	6"	—	13 cases admitted, conducting party returned, obtained 2 loads of cinders for the billet.	
"	7"	—	10 cases admitted, 16 cases transferred sick, conducting party returned.	
"	8"	—	3 cases admitted. 6 cases transferred sick	
"	9"	—	5 cases admitted. Conducting party returned. Collected two loads of ashes for the billet. No 7483 Pte O'Donnel J. proceeded to Scotland on leave from 9th to 17th of the month.	
"	10"	—	6 cases admitted. 12 cases transferred sick. Conducting party returned.	
"	11"	—	10 cases admitted. 11 cases transferred sick. The A.D.V.S. & the Vety. Officers of the Division assembled at the Section and the intra-dermal-palpebral mallein test was applied to the horses of the Section. Each V.O. doing one.	

1875 Wt. W593/826 1,000,000 4/15 J.B.C. & A. A.D.S.S./Forms/C. 2118.

Instructions regarding War Diaries and Intelligence Summaries are contained in F. S. Regs., Part II. and the Staff Manual respectively. Title Pages will be prepared in manuscript.

WAR DIARY
or
INTELLIGENCE SUMMARY
(Erase heading not required.)

Army Form C. 2118

Place	Date	Hour	Summary of Events and Information	Remarks and references to Appendices
ESTAIRES	12 12/15	—	3 cases admitted. 4 transferred sick. Conducting party returned. The result of the mallein test of yesterday is negative all round.	
"	13"	—	12 cases admitted. 7 cases transferred sick. Conducting party returned.	
"	14"	—	9 cases admitted, 13 cases transferred sick. Conducting party returned.	
"	15"	—	7 cases admitted, Conducting party returned.	
"	16"	—	6 cases transferred sick. Conducting party returned.	
"	17"	—	7 cases admitted. 7 case transferred sick. No. 80 Pte H.G. GIBBS, proceeded to England on leave from 17th to 24th of the month.	
"	18"	—	4 cases admitted. Conducting party returned.	
"	19"	—	7 cases admitted. 7 cases transferred sick. Conducting party returned. Pte O'Donnel returned delayed one day.	
"	20"	—	9 cases admitted. 6 cases transferred sick.	
"	21"	—	3 cases admitted. Conducting party returned.	
"	22"	—	4 cases admitted, 10 cases transferred sick, conducting party returned.	
"	23"	—	9 cases admitted,	
"	24"	—	8 cases admitted, 16 cases transfered sick, conducting party returned.	
"	25"	—	6 cases admitted.	
"	26"	—	4 cases admitted, 10 cases transferred sick, conducting party returned.	

1875 Wt. W593/826 1,000,000 4/15 J.B.C. & A. A.D.S.S./Forms/C. 2118.

Instructions regarding War Diaries and Intelligence Summaries are contained in F. S. Regs., Part II. and the Staff Manual respectively. Title Pages will be prepared in manuscript.

WAR DIARY
or
INTELLIGENCE SUMMARY
(Erase heading not required.)

Army Form C. 2118

Place	Date	Hour	Summary of Events and Information	Remarks and references to Appendices
ESTAIRES	27 12/15	—	17 cases admitted, 17 cases transferred sick, Pte Gibbs returned from leave having been delayed 2 days at Boulogne.	
"	28"	—	7 cases admitted, 9 cases transferred sick, conducting party returned.	
"	29"	—	16 cases admitted, 16 cases transferred sick, conducting party returned.	
"	30"	—	7 cases admitted, conducting party returned. Made arrangement with M. Huchett, NEVFBERQUIN, for the hire of a horse float at Frs 25 per week.	
"	31"	—	18 cases admitted. 24 cases transferred sick, conducting party returned.	

1875 Wt. W593/826 1,000,000 4/15 J.B.C. & A. A.D.S.S./Forms/C. 2118.

32nd Mdb: Vet: Sect:
Vol: 5

TAN

20

Instructions regarding War Diaries and Intelligence Summaries are contained in F. S. Regs., Part II. and the Staff Manual respectively. Title Pages will be prepared in manuscript.

WAR DIARY
or
INTELLIGENCE SUMMARY
(Erase heading not required.)

Army Form C. 2118

No. 32 MOBILE VETERINARY SECTION No. .... Date .... 20th DIVISION

Place	Date	Hour	Summary of Events and Information	Remarks and references to Appendices
OXELAERE	23 1/16	—	The section remained in billets which were unsatisfactory owing to the distance from Railhead. A fresh billet was taken at ARNEKE.	
"	24 1/16	—	The section marched to ARNEKE & took up a billet in a farm shown on map 5A HAZEBROUCK, 1.100,000, 3/16 of an inch due South of the R in ARNEKE. Conducting party returned.	
"	25 1/16	—	8 cases admitted.	
"	26 1/16	—	12 cases admitted. 16 cases transferred sick from ARNEKE Station to NEUF CHATEL.	
"	27 1/16	—	13 cases admitted. 11 cases transferred sick	
"	28 1/16	—	No. 6719 Pte W. BUTTERWORTH, went on leave from 28th to 3.2.16. 10 cases admitted. 11 cases transferred sick. Conducting party returned.	
"	29 1/16	—	11 cases admitted. 14 cases transferred sick. Conducting party returned. Pte LARGE returned from leave.	
"	30 1/16	—	16 cases admitted. 14 cases transferred sick. Conducting party returned.	
"	31 1/16	—	7 cases admitted. 13 cases transferred sick. SE. 2241 Pte HARLOW, A.F., A.V.C. joined the section from 'C' Battery 93rd Bde. R.F.A. having been reduced from Serjeant by F.G.C.M.	

T. Lishman,
Capt. A.V.C.
Commdg.

1875 Wt. W593/826 1,000,000 4/15 J.B.C. & A. A.D.S.S./Forms/C. 2118.

Instructions regarding War Diaries and Intelligence Summaries are contained in F. S. Regs., Part II. and the Staff Manual respectively. Title Pages will be prepared in manuscript.

WAR DIARY
or
INTELLIGENCE SUMMARY
(Erase heading not required.)

Army Form C. 2118

No 32 MOBILE VETERINARY SECTION
No.
Date
20th DIVISION

Place	Date	Hour	Summary of Events and Information	Remarks and references to Appendices
ESTAIRES	14/1/16	9 a.m.	The section paraded & marched via NEUF BERQUIN, MERVILLE, the road to LA MOTTE-AU-BOIS, LE PARC, MORBECQUE, STEENBECQUE, and into the billet on the farm of M. LYDEN WYART, Map 36A, C. 29. d. 4. 7. Arriving at 2-45 p.m. There was cover for the horses of the section, and also room for sick animals. Conducting party returned	
STEENBECQUE	15/1/16	—	1 case admitted. The men of the section employed in patching up the billet. Conducting party returned.	
"	16/1/16	—	4 cases admitted, Malleined the horses of a section of No 17 Reserve Park, & visited No 1 Section 6th Reserve Park.	
"	17/1/16	—	4 cases admitted. Got the loan of a horse float for Frs 25 per week.	
"	18/1/16	—	4 cases admitted. 11 cases transferred sick to Neuf Chatel from the railhead at STEENBECQUE.	
"	19/1/16	—	No 6538 Pte T. LARGE proceeded on 7 days special leave to England. 7 cases admitted	
"	20	—	11 cases admitted. 15 cases transferred sick. Conducting party returned.	
"	21	—	17 cases admitted. 16 cases transferred sick.	
"	22	—	7 cases admitted. 9 cases transferred sick. Conducting party returned. The section marched to OXELAERE near CASSEL.	

1875 Wt. W593/826 1,000,000 4/15 J.B.C. & A. A.D.S.S./Forms/C. 2118.

Instructions regarding War Diaries and Intelligence Summaries are contained in F. S. Regs., Part II. and the Staff Manual respectively. Title Pages will be prepared in manuscript.

WAR DIARY
or
INTELLIGENCE SUMMARY
(Erase heading not required.)

Army Form C. 2118

Place	Date	Hour	Summary of Events and Information	Remarks and references to Appendices
ESTAIRES	1/7/16	—	2 cases admitted, conducting party returned.	
"	2/7/16	—	5 cases admitted, 8 cases transferred sick. Conducting party returned. Men of Section bathed at Divisional Baths.	
"	3/7/16	—	7 cases admitted.	
"	4/7/16	—	19 cases admitted, 16 cases transferred sick, Conducting party returned.	
"	5/7/16	—	10 cases admitted, 15 cases transferred sick.	
"	6/7/16	—	4 cases admitted, conducting party returned.	
"	7/7/16	—	4 cases admitted, 7 cases transferred sick, Conducting party returned.	
"	8/7/16	—	14 cases admitted, 15 cases transferred sick.	
"	9/7/16	—	10 cases admitted, 8 cases transferred sick, Conducting party returned.	
"	10/7/16	—	11 cases admitted, Conducting party returned.	
"	11/7/16	—	13 cases admitted, Conducting party returned.	
"	12/7/16	—	12 cases admitted, 32 cases transferred sick, 2 cases died from pneumonia.	
"	13/7/16	—	3 cases transferred sick. The wagons of the Section were loaded for marching to the new billet at Steenbecque while the Division was in the training area.	

1875 Wt. W593/826 1,000,000 4/15 J.B.C. & A. A.D.S.S./Forms/C. 2118.

20

32nd Indn Vety Sectn

Vol: 6

Instructions regarding War Diaries and Intelligence Summaries are contained in F. S. Regs., Part II. and the Staff Manual respectively. Title Pages will be prepared in manuscript.

WAR DIARY
or
INTELLIGENCE SUMMARY
(Erase heading not required.)

Army Form C. 2118

No. 32 MOBILE VETERINARY SECTION
No. ....
Date ....
20th DIVISION

Place	Date	Hour	Summary of Events and Information	Remarks and references to Appendices
ARNEKE	1 2/16	—	10 cases admitted, 11 cases transferred sick, Conducting party returned.	
"	2 2/16	—	5 cases admitted, conducting party returned. One of the 5 cases admitted was found to have a fractured radius & destroyed.	
"	3 2/16	—	5 cases admitted, conducting party returned. In compliance with a wire received from the D.D.V.S., 2nd Army one limbered G.S. wagon, complete with mule & harness, was sent to Therouanne to hand over to a Sergt. A.V.C. who has to return for it a horse ambulance as a complete turnout.	
"	4 2/16	—	8 horses transferred sick, the section marched from Arneke to a billet 1 Kilometre north of LEDRINGHEM on the road from the village to WORMHOUDT.	
LEDRINGHAM	5 2/16	—	1 horse admitted. Capt. Lishman, & No 6526 Pte P.G. BRIGGS proceeded to England on leave the section coming under Maj. Steel, A.D.V.S.	
	6 2/16	—	12 cases admitted. Conducting party returned. 6719 Pte BUTTERWORTH returned from leave.	
	7 2/16	—	6 cases admitted. 13 cases transferred sick.	
	8 2/16	—	9 cases admitted. 1 case destroyed with purpura haemorrhagica.	
	9 2/16	—	12 cases admitted, 16 cases transferred sick. Conducting party returned. Men of section buried the dead horse.	

1875 Wt. W593/826 1,000,000 4/15 J.B.C. & A. A.D.S.S./Forms/C. 2118.

Army Form C. 2118

Instructions regarding War Diaries and Intelligence Summaries are contained in F. S. Regs., Part II. and the Staff Manual respectively. Title Pages will be prepared in manuscript.

WAR DIARY
or
INTELLIGENCE SUMMARY
(Erase heading not required.)

Place	Date	Hour	Summary of Events and Information	Remarks and references to Appendices
LEDRINGHEM	10 2/16	—	8 cases admitted.	
"	11 2/16	—	3 cases admitted, 8 cases transfered sick, Conducting party returned.	
"	12 2/16	—	4 cases admitted. L/Cpl. Chapman returned with a horse ambulance from ABBEVILLE to which place he had proceeded from THEROUANNE. Nº 6720 Pte S.M. BARRETT, & Nº 5802 Private J. KNOWLES proceeded to England on leave.	
"	13 2/16	—	One case admitted. 8 cases transfered sick. Conducting party returned	
"	14 2/16	—	~~[illegible]~~ Capt Lishman & Pte P.J. BRIGGS returned from leave. The Section marched to a billet near WATOU. — Sheet 27, K.5.d.8.7. Found 9 sick horses of the 14th Division in the billet which had been left that morning by Nº 26 Mobile Veterinary Section when it marched out. Three other horses from the 14th Division admitted after our arrival.	
WATOU	15 2/16	—	4 cases admitted. Conducting party returned.	
"	16 2/16	—	2 cases from 14th Div. admitted. 12 cases from 14th Div & 5 from the 20th transferred sick from POPERINGE station.	
"	17 2/16		2 cases admitted.	

Instructions regarding War Diaries and Intelligence Summaries are contained in F. S. Regs., Part II. and the Staff Manual respectively. Title Pages will be prepared in manuscript.

WAR DIARY
or
INTELLIGENCE SUMMARY
(Erase heading not required.)

Army Form C. 2118

Place	Date	Hour	Summary of Events and Information	Remarks and references to Appendices
WATOU	18 2/16	—	6 cases admitted. 1 horse of 20th D.A.C. which had been left on the march collected from Mon. Caesar Fovez, Ferme de Chateau, near STEENVOORDE.	
"	19 2/16	—	7 cases admitted.	
"	20 2/16	—	3 case admitted. 17 cases transferred sick.	
"	21 "	—	2 cases admitted. No 6720 Pte BARRETT & No 5802 Pte KNOWLES, returned from leave, & No 522 Serjt. MILLER proceeded to England on 7 days leave.	
"	22 "	—	3 cases admitted. Conducting party returned.	
"	23 "	—	8 cases admitted. 9 cases transferred sick.	
"	24 "	—	6 cases admitted.	
"	25 "	—	3 cases admitted. 10 cases transferred sick. Conducting party returned	
"	26 "	—	1 case admitted.	
"	27 "	—	3 cases admitted. 1 unknown horse collected from M. Celestine Claeuw, PROVEN, MOLENWAL. 1 case discharged cured. Conducting party returned.	
"	28 "	—	5 cases admitted.	
"	29 "	—	2 cases admitted. 8 cases transferred sick.	

No. 32 MOBILE VETERINARY SECTION No. .... Date .... 20th DIVISION

T. Lishman
Capt. A.V.C.
Comdg

1875 Wt. W593/826 1,000,000 4/15 J.B.C. & A. A.D.S.S./Forms/C. 2118.

32 MVS
Vol 7

Instructions regarding War Diaries and Intelligence Summaries are contained in F. S. Regs., Part II. and the Staff Manual respectively. Title Pages will be prepared in manuscript.

WAR DIARY
or
INTELLIGENCE SUMMARY
(Erase heading not required.)

Army Form C. 2118

Place	Date	Hour	Summary of Events and Information	Remarks and references to Appendices
WATOU	1 3/16	—	4 cases admitted, 2 cases discharged cured. No 522 Serjt J. MILLER returned from leave, delayed one day at BOULOGNE. No 6723 Pte H. CHAPMAN admitted into Hospital.	
	2 3/16	—	2 cases admitted. Conducting party returned. 1 horse discharged cured.	
	3 3/16	—	1 case admitted, 6 cases transferred sick.	
	4 3/16	—	4 cases admitted.	
	5 "	—	3 cases admitted. Conducting party returned	
	6 "	—	7 cases transferred sick	
	7 "	—	7 case admitted	
	8 "	—	4 cases admitted. Conducting party returned.	
	9 "	—	4 cases admitted, 6 cases transferred sick, 2 cases discharged cured.	
	10 "	—	1 case admitted. 1 horse discharged sick	
	11 "	—	1 case admitted. 7 cases transferred sick. Conducting party returned. O.C. Mob. Vety Sect. took over from A.D.V.S. of Div. evacuated sick.	
	12 "	—	5 cases admitted.	
	13 "	—	Handed over the Section to Capt J.B. Welham A.V.C. Took over the section. Conducting party returned	
	14	—	8 cases admitted. 4 transferred sick	

James B. Welham Capt A.V.C.

1875 Wt. W593/826 1,000,000 4/15 J.B.C. & A. A.D.S.S./Forms/C. 2118.

Army Form C. 2118

Instructions regarding War Diaries and Intelligence Summaries are contained in F. S. Regs., Part II. and the Staff Manual respectively. Title Pages will be prepared in manuscript.

WAR DIARY
or
INTELLIGENCE SUMMARY
(Erase heading not required.)

Place	Date	Hour	Summary of Events and Information	Remarks and references to Appendices
Watou	15	—	10 cases admitted	
	16	—	5 cases admitted. 20 transferred sick. Conducting party returned.	
	17	—	6 cases admitted.	
	18	—	5 cases admitted. 9 transferred sick. Conducting party returned.	
	19	—	4 cases admitted. 3 cases returned to unit, cured.	
	20	—	6 cases admitted. Conducting party returned.	
	21	—	5 cases admitted. 16 transferred sick.	
	22	—	4 cases admitted	
	23	—	7 cases admitted. Conducting party returned	
	24	—	5 cases admitted. 15 transferred sick. No 6136 Cpl. G. Patton granted leave to England 24/3/16–31/3/16.	
	25	—	3 cases admitted. 1 destroyed.	
	26	—	2 cases admitted. Conducting party returned. 9 transferred sick. Buried carcase.	
	27	—	8 cases admitted	
	28	—	7 cases admitted. Conducting party returned.	
	29	—	7 cases admitted. 11 transferred sick. 1 died.	
	30	—	8 cases admitted. 1 case returned to unit, cured. Knife section buried carcase.	
	31	—	9 cases admitted. 14 transferred sick. Conducting party returned. 1 case returned to unit, cured.	

No. 32 MOBILE VETERINARY SECTION
No. ....
Date ....
20th DIVISION

James B. Willhams Capt. A.V.C. Comdg.

1875 Wt. W593/826 1,000,000 4/15 J.B.C. & A. A.D.S.S./Forms/C. 2118.

Instructions regarding War Diaries and Intelligence Summaries are contained in F. S. Regs., Part II. and the Staff Manual respectively. Title Pages will be prepared in manuscript.

WAR DIARY
or
INTELLIGENCE SUMMARY
(Erase heading not required.)

XX

No. 32 MOBILE VETERINARY SECTION No. .... Date .... 20th DIVISION

Army Form C. 2118

32 MV Vet Sec
Vol 8

Place	Date	Hour	Summary of Events and Information April 1916	Remarks and references to Appendices
Watou	1	—	4 cases admitted.	
	2	—	9 cases admitted 15 transferred sick; 1 case cured returned to unit Conducting party returned. No 6136 Cpl. Tatton returned from leave.	
	3	—	7 cases admitted	
	4	—	6 cases admitted. 13 transferred sick. Conducting party returned.	
	5	—	10 cases admitted.	
	6	—	3 cases admitted. 14 transferred sick Conducting party returned.	
	7	—	1 case cured returned to unit.	
	8	—	1 case admitted. 1 horse destroyed. Conducting party returned.	
	9	—	9 cases admitted. No 6885 S.S. Auchterlonie J. No 6519 L/Cpl Harris J.H. leave to England.	
	10	—	13 cases admitted. 14 transferred sick 1 horse destroyed.	
	11	—	3 cases admitted, 10 transferred sick	
	12	—	5 cases admitted. Conducting party returned.	
	13	—	11 cases admitted. 12 transferred sick Conducting party returned.	
	14	—	4 cases admitted.	
	15	—	12 cases admitted 13 transferred sick Conducting party returned.	
	16	—	3 cases admitted 1 case cured returned to unit	
	17	—	5 cases admitted 10 transferred sick. Conducting party returned. 6519 L/Cpl Harris returned from leave	

Instructions regarding War Diaries and Intelligence Summaries are contained in F. S. Regs., Part II. and the Staff Manual respectively. Title Pages will be prepared in manuscript.

WAR DIARY
or
INTELLIGENCE SUMMARY
(Erase heading not required.)

No. 32 MOBILE VETERINARY SECTION No. Date. 20th DIVISION

Army Form C. 2118

Place	Date	Hour	Summary of Events and Information	Remarks and references to Appendices
Watou	18	—	10 transferred sick. Section left billet Watou & marched to new billet in rest area between Ledringhem & Wormhoudt. Took over 4 cases left behind by 11 Mobile Vety. Sec. No 6885 S.S. Auchterlonie J. returned from leave	
	19	—	1 case admitted, conducting party returned	
	20	—	1 case admitted	
	21	—	1 case admitted 5 transferred sick 1 horse destroyed.	
	22	—	1 case admitted. 1 horse returned to unit, cured.	
	23	—	Conducting party returned.	
	24	—	9 cases admitted. 1 horse collected from M. Auguste Lecomte, blacksmith, Pitgam(?).	
	25	—	6 cases admitted 10 transferred sick	
	26	—	1 case admitted. 1 horse returned to unit cured.	
	27	—	10 cases admitted. Conducting party returned	
	28	—	1 case admitted 12 transferred sick 1 case cured, returned to unit.	
	29	—	6 cases admitted 1 horse collected from M. Achille Petit, farmer of St. Laurent, Steenvoorde	
	30	—	6 cases admitted. 10 transferred sick. 2 cases returned to unit cured. No 7459 Cpl. McGuinness W.E. & No T/2 9881 Whiteley W.G. granted leave to England.	

James B. Meldrum(?) Capt. A.V.C.
Comdg.

Instructions regarding War Diaries and Intelligence Summaries are contained in F. S. Regs., Part II. and the Staff Manual respectively. Title Pages will be prepared in manuscript.

WAR DIARY
or
INTELLIGENCE SUMMARY
(Erase heading not required.)

Army Form C. 2118

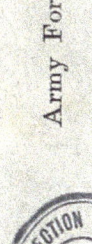

No. 32 MOBILE VETERINARY SECTION No. .... Date .... 20th DIVISION

Vol 9

Place	Date	Hour	Summary of Events and Information	Remarks and references to Appendices
[illegible]	May 1		2 cases admitted. 2 returned to unit cured. XX	
Ledringhem	2		2 cases admitted. Conducting party returned	
	3		2 cases admitted. 1 returned to unit cured.	
	4		5 cases admitted. 9 transferred sick	
	5		6 cases admitted. 1 mule collected from Camille Pockynott at Le Grand Bundles. Main Cassel/Cassel road	
	6		2 cases admitted. 1 returned to unit cured. 1 destroyed. Conducting party returned	
	7		2 cases admitted. 2 destroyed.	
	8		5 cases admitted	
	9		4 cases admitted. 4 transferred sick	
	10		2 cases admitted	
	11		2 cases admitted. Conducting party returned.	
	12		2 cases admitted. 9 transferred sick	
	14		1 case admitted. Conducting party returned.	
	15		6 cases admitted	
	16		4 cases admitted. 8 transferred sick.	
	17		8 cases admitted	
	18		7 cases admitted. Conducting party returned.	
	19		4 cases admitted. 6 transferred sick.	
	20		1 case admitted. 1 died	

1875 Wt. W593/826 1,000,000 4/15 J.B.C. & A. A.D.S.S./Forms/C. 2118.

Instructions regarding War Diaries and Intelligence Summaries are contained in F. S. Regs., Part II. and the Staff Manual respectively. Title Pages will be prepared in manuscript.

WAR DIARY
or
INTELLIGENCE SUMMARY
(Erase heading not required.)

Army Form C. 2118

Place	Date	Hour	Summary of Events and Information	Remarks and references to Appendices
Ledringhem	21		Section left billet at Ledringhem & marched to Haandoek near Poperinghe, leaving behind 5 cases to be taken over by Guards Div. Mobile Sec, & taking over from them 10. Conducting party returned.	
Haandoek	23		2 cases admitted, 8 transferred sick, & 1 mare & foal to A.R.D.	
	24		4 cases admitted.	
	25		3 cases admitted. Conducting party returned	
	26		2 cases admitted, 5 transferred sick, 1 mare in foal to A.R.D.	
	27		2 cases admitted	
	28		6 cases admitted Conducting party returned.	
	29		1 case admitted.	
	30		6 cases admitted. 19 transferred sick. 1 mule supplied to the D.A.C. posted to 60th Fd. Amb	
	31		2 cases admitted. 1 horse (stray) posted to 20th Div. P.O. Hd. Qrs	

James [illegible]
Capt A.V.C.
O.C. Comdg

1875 Wt. W593/826 1,000,000 4/15 J.B.C. & A. A.D.S.S./Forms/C. 2118.

Instructions regarding War Diaries and Intelligence Summaries are contained in F. S. Regs., Part II. and the Staff Manual respectively. Title Pages will be prepared in manuscript.

WAR DIARY
or
INTELLIGENCE SUMMARY
(Erase heading not required.)

Army Form C. 2118

XX

32 Mob Vety Sec

June

Vol 10

Place	Date	Hour	Summary of Events and Information	Remarks and references to Appendices
Hamhoek R	June 1		7 cases admitted. Conducting party returned.	
	2		2 cases admitted 9 transferred sick.	
	3		½ section inoculated.	
	4		2 cases admitted. Conducting party returned	
	5		8 cases admitted.	
	6		2 cases admitted, 12 transferred sick, 1 discharged cured	
	7		2 cases admitted, 1 discharged cured	
	8		4 cases admitted. Conducting party returned. SE/6749 Pte A. Dinnott transferred to No 4 Vety. Hospital for duty.	
	9		4 cases admitted, 10 transferred sick, 2 discharged cured.	
	10		3 cases admitted. ½ section inoculated.	
	11		1 case admitted. Conducting party returned.	
	12		2 cases & 1 stray animal admitted.	
	13		2 cases admitted 9 transferred sick.	
	14		3 cases admitted.	
	15		11 cases admitted Conducting party returned	
	16		7 cases admitted. 17 transferred sick. 1 mare & foal to A.R.D.	
	17		2 cases admitted.	
	18		4 cases admitted. Conducting party returned	
	19		9 cases admitted.	
	20		6 cases admitted 8 transferred sick 1 discharged cured.	
	21		6 cases admitted.	

Instructions regarding War Diaries and Intelligence Summaries are contained in F. S. Regs., Part II. and the Staff Manual respectively. Title Pages will be prepared in manuscript.

WAR DIARY
or
INTELLIGENCE SUMMARY
(Erase heading not required.)

Army Form C. 2118

Place	Date	Hour	Summary of Events and Information	Remarks and references to Appendices
Hamhook	22		7 cases admitted. Conducting party returned	
	23		1 case admitted. 16 transferred sick, 1 died.	
	24		4 cases admitted.	
	25		2 cases admitted. 8 transferred sick, 1 (vice) to A.R.D. These evacuated by road. Conducting party returned.	
	26		6 cases admitted	
	27		2 cases admitted 8 transferred sick	
	28		4 cases admitted Road conducting party returned	
	29		6 cases admitted	
	30		2 cases admitted. Stray horse posted to No. 1 Section D.A.C.	

1875 Wt. W593/826 1,000,000 4/15 J.B.C. & A. A.D.S.S./Forms/C. 2118.

Instructions regarding War Diaries and Intelligence Summaries are contained in F. S. Regs., Part II. and the Staff Manual respectively. Title Pages will be prepared in manuscript.

WAR DIARY
or ~~INTELLIGENCE SUMMARY~~ of
(Erase heading not required.)

Army Form C. 2118

July

32 Mob. Vet. Sect. Vol 11

Place	Date	Hour	Summary of Events and Information	Remarks and references to Appendices
Hamhock	July 1		8 cases admitted	
	2		2 cases admitted. 10 transferred sick. 1 to A.R.D. 1 discharged cured.	
	3		6 cases admitted. 1 died.	
	4		6 cases admitted.	
	5		1 case admitted. 4 transferred to A.R.D. 1 cured. Conducting party returned.	
	6		7 cases admitted.	
	7		14 cases admitted. 1 destroyed	
	8		3 cases admitted.	
	9		3 cases admitted. 32 transferred sick & 1 discharged cured	
	10		6 cases admitted.	
	11		5 cases admitted.	
	12		12 cases admitted. 1 died. Conducting party returned	
	13		4 cases admitted. 1 destroyed	
	14		8 cases admitted. 15 transferred sick. 1 discharged cured. 1 destroyed.	
	15		12 cases admitted. 3 discharged cured.	
	16		5 cases admitted. 22 transferred sick. 1 discharged cured. Conducting party returned.	
	17		1 case admitted. Handed over 10 cases to 6th Mobile Vety. Sec. & moved to Ledringhem.	
Ledringhem	18		Conducting party returned.	
	19		2 cases admitted	

1875 Wt. W593/826 1,000,000 4/15 J.B.C. & A. A.D.S.S./Forms/C.

Instructions regarding War Diaries and Intelligence Summaries are contained in F. S. Regs., Part II. and the Staff Manual respectively. Title Pages will be prepared in manuscript.

WAR DIARY
or
INTELLIGENCE SUMMARY
(Erase heading not required.)

Army Form C. 2118

Place	Date	Hour	Summary of Events and Information	Remarks and references to Appendices
Ledringhem	20		Section marched to Bailleul (N)	
	21		2 admitted. 12 transferred sick. Section marched to Bailleul (S) & took over billet of 46th Mob. Vety. Sec.	
	22		4 cases admitted. Conducting party returned	
	23		Section marched to St. Sylvester Cappel	
	24		2 admitted	
	25		Left 2 cases at billet, marched to Bavinchove, entrained to Doullens & marched to billet at Grouches	
	26		Marched to Couin	
	28		18 admitted	
	29		13 admitted. Marched to St Leger-les-Authie	
	30		18 transferred sick, 2 admitted	
	31		5 cases admitted 9 transferred sick	

James B. [illegible]
Capt. A.V.C.
O.C.

No. 32 MOBILE VETERINARY SECTION
No. ....
Date 31.7.16
20th DIVISION

WAR DIARY
or
INTELLIGENCE SUMMARY
(Erase heading not required.)

Instructions regarding War Diaries and Intelligence Summaries are contained in F. S. Regs., Part II. and the Staff Manual respectively. Title Pages will be prepared in manuscript.

32 Mob. Vet. Sec.

Vol 12

August 1916

Place	Date	Hour	Summary of Events and Information	Remarks and references to Appendices
[illegible] [illegible]	1		[illegible] Cases admitted. Collected 2 horses from inhabitants.	
	2		[illegible] Cases admitted	
	3		7 Cases admitted 13 transferred sick. Collected 1 horse from inhabitants.	
	4		7 Cases admitted.	
	5		8 Cases admitted. 10 transferred sick. Conducting party returned	
	6		2 Cases admitted. 12 transferred sick & 2 [illegible]	
	7		14 Cases admitted. 14 transferred sick. Conducting party returned	
	8		[illegible] Cases admitted. Conducting party returned	
	9		[illegible] Cases admitted 13 transferred sick 16 [illegible] [illegible] conducting party returned	
	10		5 Cases admitted	
	11		[illegible] Cases admitted. Conducting party returned	
	12		[illegible] Cases admitted 25 transferred sick. 2 [illegible] [illegible]	
	13		8 Cases admitted	
	14		3 Cases admitted 1 died. Conducting party returned	
	15		[illegible] Cases admitted. 12 transferred sick. 2 cured	
	16		[illegible] Cases admitted 1 cured	

1875 Wt. W593/826 1,000,000 4/15 J.B.C. & A. A.D.S.S./Forms/C. 2118.

Instructions regarding War Diaries and Intelligence Summaries are contained in F. S. Regs., Part II. and the Staff Manual respectively. Title Pages will be prepared in manuscript.

WAR DIARY
or
INTELLIGENCE SUMMARY
(Erase heading not required.)

Place	Date	Hour	Summary of Events and Information	Remarks and references to Appendices
[illegible]	17		Handed over 9 sick animals to 36th Mobile Vety. Sec. Unit marched to [illegible]	
[illegible]				
[illegible]	18		Unit marched to [illegible]	
[illegible]	19		Unit marched to [illegible]	
[illegible]	20		Unit marched to [illegible]. Conducting party returned	
[illegible]	21		Unit marched to [illegible]	
[illegible]	22		Unit marched to [illegible]	
[illegible]	23		Took over advanced dressing station from 36th Mobile Vety. Sec.	
	24		4 cases admitted. 1 cured	
	25		3 cases admitted	
	26		3 cases admitted. 10 transferred sick	
	27		2 cases admitted	
	28		4 cases admitted. Conducting party returned	
	29		2 cases admitted. 10 transferred sick	
	30		1 admitted. 1 destroyed	
	31		Conducting party returned	

James C. Wallace
Capt. A.V.C.
OC 32nd Mob. Vety. Sec.

Instructions regarding War Diaries and Intelligence Summaries are contained in F. S. Regs., Part II. and the Staff Manual respectively. Title Pages will be prepared in manuscript.

WAR DIARY
or
INTELLIGENCE SUMMARY
(Erase heading not required.)

32 Mobile Veterinary Section.

Army Form C. 2118

Vol 13

Place	Date	Hour	Summary of Events and Information Sept 1916	Remarks and references to Appendices
Meaulte	1st Sept.		9 cases admitted	
	2		7 cases admitted. 21 transferred sick.	
	3		2 cases admitted	
	4		10 cases admitted. Conducting party returned.	
	5		14 cases admitted. 24 transferred sick 1 returned to unit cured	
	6		12 cases admitted 15 transferred sick 4 handed over to 46th M.V.S. 1 returned to unit cured	
Corbie	7		Unit marched to Corbie	
			Dr Whitsky A.S.C. admitted to hospital, suffering from kick from mule. Conducting party returned.	
	9		One case admitted.	
	10		4 cases admitted	
Meaulte	11		Unit marched to Meaulte.	
	12		One case admitted.	
	13		6 cases admitted.	
	14		2 cases admitted 4 transferred sick.	
	15		9 cases admitted. 2 transferred sick	
	16		6 cases admitted 3 transferred sick. Conducting party returned.	
	17		2 cases admitted.	

1875 Wt. W593/826 1,000,000 4/15 J.B.C. & A. A.D.S.S./Forms/C. 2118.

Army Form C. 2118

Instructions regarding War Diaries and Intelligence Summaries are contained in F. S. Regs., Part II. and the Staff Manual respectively. Title Pages will be prepared in manuscript.

WAR DIARY
or
INTELLIGENCE SUMMARY
(Erase heading not required.)

Place	Date	Hour	Summary of Events and Information	Remarks and references to Appendices
Meaulte	19	Sept	2 cases admitted. 4 transferred sick.	
	20		3 cases admitted.	
	21		2 cases admitted. 4 transferred sick.	
	22		7 cases admitted. 4 transferred sick.	
	23		6 cases admitted. 6 transferred sick.	
	24		6 cases admitted. 6 transferred sick.	
	25		6 cases admitted. 3 transferred sick.	
	26		7 cases admitted. 4 transferred sick. 1 returned to unit cured.	
	27		3 cases admitted. 5 transferred sick. No T/31533 Pte. A. Ross A.S.C. joined the section.	
	28		3 cases admitted.	
	29		6 cases admitted. 8 transferred sick.	
	30		Advance collecting station opened at CARNOY.	

32 MOBILE VETERINARY SECTION
No. ....
Date ....
20th DIVISION

James [illegible]
Capt. A.V.C.
O.C. 32 M.V.S.

1875 Wt. W593/826 1,000,000 4/15 J.B.C. & A. A.D.S.S./Forms/C. 2118.

Vol 14

32nd Mobile Vet. Section. 20 Div

October 1916

Army Form C. 2118

Instructions regarding War Diaries and Intelligence Summaries are contained in F. S. Regs., Part II. and the Staff Manual respectively. Title Pages will be prepared in manuscript.

WAR DIARY
or
INTELLIGENCE SUMMARY
(Erase heading not required.)

Place	Date	Hour	Summary of Events and Information	Remarks and references to Appendices
Méaulte	1 Oct.		17 cases admitted, 42 transferred sick. 1 died	
	2		16 admitted, 17 transferred sick.	
	3		17 admitted, 15 transferred sick.	
	4		16 admitted, 13 transferred sick, 2 died	
	5		24 admitted.	
	6		28 admitted, 37 transferred sick, 1 died.	
	7		36 admitted 23 transferred sick, 1 returned to unit cured.	
	8		28 admitted, 26 transferred sick, 1 died.	
	9		32 admitted 29 transferred sick, 1 died.	
	10		13 admitted 39 transferred sick, 1 returned to unit cured, 1 destroyed	
	11		35 admitted, 16 transferred sick, 1 returned to unit cured.	
	12		22 cases admitted 16 transferred sick, 1 returned to unit cured.	
	13		22 admitted, 24 transferred sick, 1 returned to unit cured	
	14		15 cases admitted, 31 transferred sick, 1 returned to unit cured.	
	15		1 case admitted, 8 transferred sick. Unit marched to Corbie.	

1875 Wt. W593/826 1,000,000 4/15 J.B.C. & A. A.D.S.S./Forms/C. 2118.

Instructions regarding War Diaries and Intelligence Summaries are contained in F. S. Regs., Part II. and the Staff Manual respectively. Title Pages will be prepared in manuscript.

WAR DIARY
or
INTELLIGENCE SUMMARY
(Erase heading not required.)

Army Form C. 2118

Place	Date	Hour	Summary of Events and Information	Remarks and references to Appendices
Corbie	16		5 cases admitted. Collected 2 animals from inhabitants left behind by 36 Div	
	18		3 cases admitted. 4 sent to Field Remount Section, 4th Army. 1 N.C.O. & 5 men transferred for duty to 6th Mob. Vety. Sec	
	19		1 case admitted. 9 transferred sick. Unit marched to Vignacourt.	
	21		Unit marched to Bolloy sur Somme	
	22		4 cases admitted. Collected 1 mule from inhabitant that had been left, unable to march	
	23		7 cases admitted.	
	24		1 admitted. 8 sick & 2 French stray horses transferred to L of C	
	25		8 cases admitted. 1 returned to duty cured	
	26/27		1 case admitted. 6 transferred sick	
	28		1 case admitted	
	29		1 admitted.	
	30		4 admitted. Collected 1 horse from inhabitant, that had been left unable to march	
	31		6 transferred sick, 2 collected from inhabitant unable to march	

James B. Wallace
Capt. A.V.C.
O.C.

No. 32 MOBILE VETERINARY SECTION
No. 31/8/16
Date
20th DIVISION

1875 Wt. W593/826 1,000,000 4/15 J.B.C. & A. A.D.S.S./Forms/C. 2118.

Instructions regarding War Diaries and Intelligence Summaries are contained in F. S. Regs., Part II. and the Staff Manual respectively. Title Pages will be prepared in manuscript.

WAR DIARY
or
INTELLIGENCE SUMMARY
(Erase heading not required.)

Army Form C. 2118

Mob Vety Sec
Vol 15

Place	Date	Hour	Summary of Events and Information	Remarks and references to Appendices
~~Corbie~~ BELLOY-SUR-SOMME	1/11/16		Marched to Oissy	
	3/11/16		1. Horse admitted	
	4/11/16		3. Cases admitted, 2 Cases Collected from Argoeves.	
	5/11/16		5. Cases admitted, 2. Cases collected from Argoeves, 1 Case from Ailly Sur Somme.	
	6/11/16		2. Cases admitted	
	7th		12. Cases transferred to L. of C., 1. Case Cured, 1 Case destroyed at Argoeves. Sergt. Anthony and Pte Butterworth returned from No. 15. M.V.S. 8 Div., escort to Ptes Gilbey and Knowles No. 80. Pte Gibbs transferred to No 2 M.V.S., 1st Div.	
	9th		5. Cases admitted, 1. Stray Case collected at St Sauveur. No. 6538. Pte Large transferred to A.V.C. Base Depot, Havre.	
	10th		2. Cases admitted	
	11th		3. Remounts returned to Units.	
	13th		4 Cases admitted.	
	14th		9. Cases transferred to L of C. No. 6753. Pte H Phillipps transferred to A.V.C. Base Depot, Havre.	
Ailly s	15th		Marched to Ailly Sur Somme	
Corbie	16th		Marched to Corbie.	

1875 Wt. W593/826 1,000,000 4/15 J.B.C. & A. A.D.S.S./Forms/C. 2118.

Instructions regarding War Diaries and Intelligence Summaries are contained in F. S. Regs., Part II. and the Staff Manual respectively. Title Pages will be prepared in manuscript.

WAR DIARY
or
INTELLIGENCE SUMMARY
(Erase heading not required.)

Army Form C. 2118

Place	Date	Hour	Summary of Events and Information	Remarks and references to Appendices
Corbie	17.		No. 1282 Pte Gilbey and No 5802 Pte Knowles were tried by F. G. Courts Martial and found Guilty of Drunkeness and Resisting escort, were awarded 35 days F. P. No 1. and fined £1. each.	
	19.		7. Cases admitted	
	20.		2. Cases admitted, 1. Case destroyed and stray horse collected from St Sauveur on 9/11/16 handed over to 84th Field Co R.E.	
	21.		2. Cases admitted, No 7441. Pte H. Ashley, No 4020 Pte C. H. Maunder, No 1399. Pte Rallings, No. 3643. Pte F. L. Saunders and No 1507 Pte E. Waite were transferred to this Unit from No. 10. Vet. Hosp. Neufchatel. Sergt. Anthony and Ptes Davis and Knight were sent to No 18 M.V.S. 29th Div. for Duty.	
	22.		1. Case admitted, Corpl. Yeo and Ptes Barrett, Gilbey and Knowles were transferred to No 10. Vet. Hosp. Neufchatel.	
	23.		4. Cases admitted, 9 Cases transferred to L. of C. Pte O'Donnell returned from No 18 M.V.S.	
	24		16. Cases admitted, Pte O'Donnell transferred to No 10. Vet. Hosp. Neufchatel. Collected 5 Cases from Bonnay	

1875 Wt. W593/826 1,000,000 4/15 J.B.C. & A. A.D.S.S./Forms/C. 2118.

Instructions regarding War Diaries and Intelligence Summaries are contained in F. S. Regs., Part II. and the Staff Manual respectively. Title Pages will be prepared in manuscript.

WAR DIARY
or
INTELLIGENCE SUMMARY
(Erase heading not required.)

Army Form C. 2118

Place	Date	Hour	Summary of Events and Information	Remarks and references to Appendices
Corbie	25		9. Cases admitted, 18 cases transferred to L. of C., Collected 1 Case from Bonnay	
	26.		5. Cases admitted, 12 Cases transferred to L. of C., Collected 1 Case from Noyelles.	
	27		19 Cases admitted, Collected to Cases from Bonnay.	
	28		18 Cases admitted, 22 Cases transferred to L. of C. No. 564. Pte J. Knight and No. 10332. Pte A. G. Nash, were transferred to this unit from No. 19. Vet Hosp.	
	29		25 Cases admitted, 18 cases transferred to L of C., Collected 5 Cases from La Neuville and one Case from Bonnay.	
	30		31 Cases admitted, 22 Cases transferred to L. of C. Collected 3 Cases from Bussy les Daours.	

W. Denington
Capt. A.V.C.

1875 Wt. W593/826 1,000,000 4/15 J.B.C. & A. A.D.S.S./Forms/C. 2118.

Instructions regarding War Diaries and Intelligence Summaries are contained in F. S. Regs., Part II. and the Staff Manual respectively. Title Pages will be prepared in manuscript.

WAR DIARY
or
INTELLIGENCE SUMMARY
(Erase heading not required.)

Army Form C. 2118

Mob Vety Sec
Vol 16

Place	Date	Hour	Summary of Events and Information	Remarks and references to Appendices
Corbie	Dec 1		4 cases admitted, 36 cases transferred sick.	
	2		11 admitted. Collected 2 animals from inhabitant at Bussy les Daours	
	3		8 admitted. 13 transferred sick. Collected horse from 9 Reserve Park A.S.C. at Daours left by 51 Batt. 913th Bde. R.F.A.	
	4		5 cases admitted. 1 died.	
	5		5 cases admitted. 10 transferred sick. Collected 2 animals from inhabitant at DAOURS.	
	6		18 admitted. 1 destroyed. Collected 2 animals from inhabitant at DAOURS.	
	7		7 cases admitted, 18 transferred sick	
	8		6 admitted.	
	9		11 admitted; 8 transferred sick, 2 to A.R.D. Collected one horse from inhabitant at BONNAY	
	10		3 admitted. 1 returned to unit cured.	
	11		3 cases admitted; 17 transferred sick	
CARNOY.	12		Unit marched to CARNOY. Handed over to 18th M.V.S., 29th Div at CORBIE 4 animals.	
	14		29 animals admitted.	
	15		5 admitted, 25 transferred sick.	
	16		33 cases admitted	

Army Form C. 2118

Instructions regarding War Diaries and Intelligence Summaries are contained in F. S. Regs., Part II. and the Staff Manual respectively. Title Pages will be prepared in manuscript.

WAR DIARY
or
INTELLIGENCE SUMMARY
(Erase heading not required.)

Place	Date	Hour	Summary of Events and Information	Remarks and references to Appendices
CARNOY	17		5 admitted; 14 transferred sick	
	18		7 cases admitted. 1 destroyed.	
	19		5 cases admitted. 10 transferred sick.	
	20		11 cases admitted. 1 destroyed, 1 returned to unit cured.	
	21		20 cases admitted. 1 died.	
	22		23 cases admitted. 30 transferred sick. 1 destroyed.	
	23		20 cases admitted. 28 transferred sick; 1 returned to unit cured. 1 destroyed	
	24		1 case admitted. 16 transferred sick. 1 returned to unit cured.	
CORBIE	25		Unit marched to CORBIE. Relieved by 29th M.V.S., 17th Div. to which were attached 1 N.C.O. & 3 men.	
	26		4 cases admitted.	
	27		3 cases transferred sick.	
	28		6 cases admitted.	
	29		6 cases admitted. 8 transferred sick. 2 to A.R.D.	
	30		13 cases admitted.	
	31		3 cases admitted. 18 transferred sick. 2 to A.R.D. 1 animal collected from inhabitant at AMIENS.	

1875 Wt. W593/826 1,000,000 4/15 J.B.C. & A. A.D.S.S./Forms/C. 2118.

32 Mobile Veterinary Section. A.V.C.

Nominal Roll of Officers possessing Chemical experience:-

Nil.

James B. [illegible]

Capt. A.V.C.
O.C.

No. 32 MOBILE VETERINARY SECTION
No. ....
Date 1. 1. 17
20th DIVISION

Establishment of Animals 31.12.16.

as per D.D. Remounts, 4th Army, No 4/3/1 20 Division No Q/20/4141/36.

Formation	Unit's Strength					Totals.					Remarks.
	Riders.	Draught.	H.D.	Pack	Total	Riders	Draught.	H.D.	Pack.	Total.	
32 Mobile Vety. Section	20	4 Mules	-	~~4 Mules~~	24	20	4 Mules	-	-	~~24~~	
Attached from 158 Coy A.S.C.	-	-	2	-	2	-	-	2		2	DIVL. TRAIN.
Totals	20	4 Mules	2	-	26	20	4 Mules	2	-	26	

No. 32 MOBILE VETERINARY SECTION
No. ....
Dat 31.12.16
... DIVISION

James B. Gillham

Capt. A.V.C.
O.C.

Establishment of Animals 31.12.16.

as per D.D Remounts, 4th Army. No 4/3/1 20 Division No Q/20/4141/36.

Formation	Units Strength					Totals					Remarks
	Riders.	Draughts	H.D	Pack	Total	Riders	Draughts.	H.D.	Pack	Total	
32 Mobile Very Section	20	4 Mules	-	4 Mules	24	20	4 Mules	-		24	
Attached from 158 Coy A.S.C	-		2	-	2	-	-	2		.2	DIVL. TRAIN
Totals	20	4 Mules	2	-	26	20	4 Mules	2	-	26	

James B [illegible]

Capt A.V.C.
O.C.

Vol 17

WAR DIARY

of the

32nd MOBILE VET. SECTION

January 1917.

Instructions regarding War Diaries and Intelligence Summaries are contained in F. S. Regs., Part II. and the Staff Manual respectively. Title Pages will be prepared in manuscript.

WAR DIARY
or
INTELLIGENCE SUMMARY
(Erase heading not required.)

Army Form C. 2118

Place	Date	Hour	Summary of Events and Information	Remarks and references to Appendices
CORBIE	Jan 1, 1917		14 cases admitted.	
	2		6 admitted, 21 transferred sick.	
	3		31 cases admitted	
	4		14 admitted, 31 transferred sick. ~~[illegible]~~ 1 handed over to 46 M.V.S. Unit marched to CARNOY. 1 relieved 46th Mob. Vety. Sec	
CARNOY	5		51 animals admitted 28 transferred sick	
	6		12 admitted, 34 transferred sick. 2 destroyed. No 15244 S.S. Day, William joined unit from No 2 Vety. Hospital	
	7		10 cases admitted. No 6885 S.S. Auchterlonie transferred to School of Farriery, Abbeville	
	8		53 cases admitted. 51 transferred sick. 1 returned to unit, cured	
	9		39 admitted, 56 transferred sick	
	10		9 cases admitted, 16 transferred sick	
	11		15 cases admitted, 21 transferred sick	
	12		9 cases admitted.	
	13		6 admitted, 16 transferred sick, 1 destroyed	
	14		13 cases admitted	
	15		14 admitted, 31 transferred sick	
	16		10 cases admitted	

1875 Wt. W593/826 1,000,000 4/15 J.B.C. & A. A.D.S.S./Forms/C. 2118.

Army Form C. 2118

Instructions regarding War Diaries and Intelligence Summaries are contained in F. S. Regs., Part II. and the Staff Manual respectively. Title Pages will be prepared in manuscript.

WAR DIARY
or
INTELLIGENCE SUMMARY
(Erase heading not required.)

Place	Date	Hour	Summary of Events and Information	Remarks and references to Appendices
CARNOY	17		18 admitted, 24 transferred sick.	
	18		12 admitted.	
	19		1 admitted, 17 transferred sick, 1 destroyed. No 11808 Pte Gowan A. joined from No 2 Vety Hospital.	
	20		7 admitted.	
	21		31 admitted, 36 transferred sick.	
	22		4 admitted. No 3943 Pte Folly A. joined from No 2 Vety. Hospital.	
	23		9 admitted 1 destroyed	
	24		3 admitted, 19 transferred sick 7 returned to units, cured.	
	25		8 admitted.	
	26		4 admitted, 13 transferred sick, 1 returned to unit, cured.	
	27		3 cases handed over to 29th M.V.S. Unit marched from CARNOY to HEILLY	
	28		2 admitted.	
	29		1 admitted.	
	30		3 admitted.	
	31		2 admitted	

No 32 MOBILE VETERINARY SECTION
No. ....
Date 31.1.17
DIVISION

James B. Milhane
Capt. A.V.C.
O.C.

1875 Wt. W593/826 1,000,000 4/15 J.B.C. & A. A.D.S.S./Forms/C. 2118.

War Diary Vol 18

of

32nd Mob. Vet. Section
20th Division

February 1917

Instructions regarding War Diaries and Intelligence Summaries are contained in F. S. Regs., Part II. and the Staff Manual respectively. Title Pages will be prepared in manuscript.

WAR DIARY
or
INTELLIGENCE SUMMARY
(Erase heading not required.)

Army Form C. 2118

Place	Date	Hour	Summary of Events and Information	Remarks and references to Appendices
	Feb.			
HEILLY	2		4 cases admitted.	
	3		3 admitted. No 3943 Pte. A. Folly admitted to hospital.	
	4		11 admitted. 3 destroyed.	
	5		1 admitted.	
	6		4 admitted. 1 died.	
	7		1 admitted.	
CARNOY.	9		Section marched to CARNOY, relieved at HEILLY by 18th M.V.S., 29th Div. Handed over to them 25 sick. 1 died & 1 was destroyed on this day. 18th M.V.S. handed over to this Unit 24 sick.	
	10		2 admitted.	
			1 case admitted.	
	11		3 destroyed.	
	12		2 admitted.	
	13		7 admitted. 27 transferred sick. 2 destroyed.	
	14		20 admitted	

Instructions regarding War Diaries and Intelligence Summaries are contained in F. S. Regs., Part II. and the Staff Manual respectively. Title Pages will be prepared in manuscript.

WAR DIARY
or
INTELLIGENCE SUMMARY
(Erase heading not required.)

Army Form C. 2118

Place	Date	Hour	Summary of Events and Information	Remarks and references to Appendices
CARNOY	15		1 admitted	
	16		11 admitted	
	17		3 admitted. Pte A. Folley No 3943 invalided to England.	
	19		1 admitted. 4 destroyed	
	20		35 transferred sick. 1 (Vice) to A.R.D. No 959 Pte F. Coyle joined the Section from No 19th Vety. Hospital	
	22		1 case admitted. 1 stray admitted.	
	23		6 cases admitted.	
	24		1 case admitted. 9 transferred sick.	
	25		4 admitted also 1 stray.	
	26		18 admitted.	
	27		1 admitted. 20 transferred sick.	

James B. Wallace
Capt A.V.C.

Vol 19

WAR DIARY

OF

32nd Mobile VETERINARY SECTION

MARCH 1917

Army Form C. 2118

Instructions regarding War Diaries and Intelligence Summaries are contained in F. S. Regs., Part II. and the Staff Manual respectively. Title Pages will be prepared in manuscript.

WAR DIARY
or
INTELLIGENCE SUMMARY
(Erase heading not required.)

Place	Date	Hour	Summary of Events and Information	Remarks and references to Appendices
CARNOY	Mar 2		27 cases admitted.	
	3		5 admitted, 27 transferred sick.	
	4		1 admitted.	
	5		52 admitted.	
	6		50 transferred sick, 1 died, 1 destroyed.	
	7		1 admitted. No 4030 Pte. Saunders admitted to 84th Fd Ambulance & evacuated to 34 C.C.S.	
	9		15 admitted	
	10		4 admitted. 19 transferred sick. No 17021 S.S. Clark. H. joined from No 9 Vety. Hospital.	
	11		1 admitted. N.M.C.	
	12		25 admitted.	
	13		3 admitted. 27 transferred sick. 2 destroyed.	
	16		26 admitted. No 15244 S.S. Day. W. left unit for School of Shoeing, Abbeville	
	17		2 admitted. 36 transferred sick 2 destroyed.	
	19		50 admitted. 2 returned to unit cured.	

1875 Wt. W593/826 1,000,000 4/15 J.B.C. & A. A.D.S.S./Forms/C. 2118.

Army Form C. 2118

Instructions regarding War Diaries and Intelligence Summaries are contained in F. S. Regs., Part II. and the Staff Manual respectively. Title Pages will be prepared in manuscript.

WAR DIARY
or
INTELLIGENCE SUMMARY
(Erase heading not required.)

Place	Date	Hour	Summary of Events and Information	Remarks and references to Appendices
CARNOY	Mar 20		2 cases admitted. 40 transferred sick 1 died.	
BRIQUETERIE	21		19 admitted. Unit marched to the BRIQUETERIE, North of MARICOURT. Cpl. Nairn on special leave to England.	
	22		9 admitted	
	23		1 admitted.	
	24		30 transferred sick 1 died.	
	26		16 admitted	
	27		16 transferred sick. 522 S/Sergt. Miller left unit for No 19 Vety. Hospital	
	28		3 admitted. 1 died	
	29		2 destroyed. No 4427 Pte. Harvey D. joined from No 3 Vety. Hospital.	
	30		14 admitted.	
	31		14 transferred sick.	

James B[illegible] Capt. A.V.C.
O.C. 32 M.V.S.

1875 Wt. W593/826 1,000,000 4/15 J.B.C. & A. A.D.S.S./Forms/C. 2118.

War Diary Vol 20

32nd Mobile Veterinary Section

April 1917

Instructions regarding War Diaries and Intelligence Summaries are contained in F. S. Regs., Part II. and the Staff Manual respectively. Title Pages will be prepared in manuscript.

WAR DIARY
or
INTELLIGENCE SUMMARY
(Erase heading not required.)

Army Form C. 2118

Place	Date	Hour	Summary of Events and Information	Remarks and references to Appendices
BRIQUETERIE	Apr 2		18 cases admitted.	
	3		1 admitted, 19 transferred sick.	
LE TRANSLOY	4		Unit moved to LE TRANSLOY	
	6		20 cases admitted.	
	7		20 transferred sick.	
	9		22 admitted.	
	10		3 admitted, 22 transferred sick.	
	12		1 admitted.	
	13		8 admitted, 1 died, 1 destroyed.	
	14		5 admitted. 11 transferred sick, 1 returned to unit cured	
	15		1 destroyed	
	16		5 cases admitted, 1 stray animal brought in.	
	17		5 admitted. 13 transferred sick.	
	18		1 admitted.	

1875 Wt. W593/826 1,000,000 4/15 J.B.C. & A. A.D.S.S./Forms/C. 2118.

Instructions regarding War Diaries and Intelligence Summaries are contained in F. S. Regs., Part II. and the Staff Manual respectively. Title Pages will be prepared in manuscript.

WAR DIARY
or
INTELLIGENCE SUMMARY
(Erase heading not required.)

Army Form C. 2118

Place	Date	Hour	Summary of Events and Information	Remarks and references to Appendices
LE TRANSLOY		20/4	11 cases admitted 1 destroyed	
		21	10 transferred sick	
		23	6 admitted. 1 returned to unit cured. 1 Cpl & 3 men withdrawn to form Corps M.V.S.	
		24	2 admitted. 7 transferred sick. 1 stray animal brought in	
		25	1 returned to unit cured. No 3131 Pte. FILBY R.K. A.V.C. joined from No 6 Vety. Hospital	
		27	5 admitted. Unit marched to ROCQUIGNY	
ROCQUIGNY		28	5 transferred sick	
		29	1 case admitted. No 15244 S.S. DAY A.V.C. returned to unit from School of Farriery, Abbeville	
		30	2 cases admitted.	

James B Chilham Capt. A.V.C. (T.C.)
O.C. 32 M.V.S.

1875 Wt. W593/826 1,000,000 4/15 J.B.C. & A. A.D.S.S./Forms/C. 2118.

WAR DIARY Vol 21

MAY 1917

32nd Mobile Veterinary Section

Instructions regarding War Diaries and Intelligence Summaries are contained in F. S. Regs., Part II. and the Staff Manual respectively. Title pages will be prepared in manuscript.

WAR DIARY
or
INTELLIGENCE SUMMARY.
(Erase heading not required.)

Army Form C. 2118.

Place	Date	Hour	Summary of Events and Information	Remarks and references to Appendices
ROCQUIGNY	May 1		1 case admitted 7 transferred sick	
	2		2 admitted.	
	3		1 admitted	
	4		1 admitted No 17021 S S Clark A.V.C. despatched to No 2 Vety Hospital	
	5		1 admitted.	
	6		3 admitted, 1 returned to unit cured	
	7		6 admitted.	
	8		13 transferred sick.	
	9		1 admitted.	
	11		8 admitted	
	12		2 admitted. 6 transferred sick	
	14		22 admitted. 1 returned to unit cured	
	15		17 admitted. 38 transferred sick.	
	18		29 admitted	
	19		31 transferred sick.	
	20		1 admitted. 1 returned to unit cured.	

A5834 Wt. W4973/M687 750,000 8/16 D. D. & L. Ltd. Forms/C.2118/13.

Instructions regarding War Diaries and Intelligence Summaries are contained in F. S. Regs., Part II. and the Staff Manual respectively. Title pages will be prepared in manuscript.

WAR DIARY
or
INTELLIGENCE SUMMARY.
(Erase heading not required.)

Army Form C. 2118.

Place	Date	Hour	Summary of Events and Information	Remarks and references to Appendices
ROCQUIGNY	21		1 case admitted	
	22		1 returned to unit cured	
	23		Unit to H21a 2.7 (Sheet 57c) Relieved by 19th M.V.S. 42nd Div (handed over one horse) &	
BAPAUME			took over from M.V.S. of 5th Australian Division	
	24		Cpl. Harris & 3 men returned from 13th Corps M.V. Detachment	
	27		1 admitted	
	28		4 admitted	
	29		5 admitted 1 returned to unit cured	
	30		2 admitted	
	31		7 admitted 1 returned to unit cured. Unit moved to H21c 2.2 (Sheet 57c)	

32ND MOBILE VETERINARY SECTION, 20TH DIVISION. 31.5.17.

James Blackhouse Capt AVC O.C.

A5834 Wt. W4973/M687 750,000 8/16 D. D. & L. Ltd. Forms/C.2118/13.

WAR DIARY
OF
32ND MOBILE
VETY SECT

JUNE 1917

Vol 22

Army Form C. 2118.

Instructions regarding War Diaries and Intelligence Summaries are contained in F. S. Regs., Part II. and the Staff Manual respectively. Title pages will be prepared in manuscript.

WAR DIARY
or
INTELLIGENCE SUMMARY.
(Erase heading not required.)

Place	Date	Hour	Summary of Events and Information	Remarks and references to Appendices
	June 1		2 cases admitted, 15 transferred sick, 1 died.	
	2		1 stray L.D. returned to 10 K.R.R.	
	3		2 cases returned to unit cured.	
	4		1 admitted. Section moved to FAVREUIL.	
	5		3 admitted. 2 returned to unit cured.	
	6		3 admitted	
	7		4 admitted	
	8		19 transferred sick	
	11		4 admitted	
	12		4 admitted	
	16		1 admitted	
	18		6 admitted	
	19		10 transferred sick. 1 stray mule issued to No 1 section 20 D.A.C	
	21		6 admitted	
	22		3 admitted. 1 returned to unit cured.	
	23		1 admitted	

A5834 Wt. W4973/M687 750,000 8/16 D. D. & L. Ltd. Forms/C.2118/13.

Instructions regarding War Diaries and Intelligence Summaries are contained in F. S. Regs., Part II. and the Staff Manual respectively. Title pages will be prepared in manuscript.

WAR DIARY
or
INTELLIGENCE SUMMARY.
(Erase heading not required.)

Army Form C. 2118.

Place	Date	Hour	Summary of Events and Information	Remarks and references to Appendices
	25		4 cases admitted	
	26		10 transferred sick	
	27		2 admitted	
	28		2 admitted.	
	29		Section marched to ACHEUX. Handed over 2 animals to 2/1 West Riding M.V.S. 62nd Div.	
	30		Section marched to BERNAVILLE	

James B Kelham
Capt. A.V.C.
6 C.

82ND MOBILE VETERINARY SECTION, 20TH DIVISION.
No. ....
Date ....

A5834 · Wt. W4973/M687 750,000 8/16 D. D. & L. Ltd. Forms/C.2118/13.

Vol 23

War Diary

32 M V Section

July 1917

Instructions regarding War Diaries and Intelligence Summaries are contained in F. S. Regs., Part II. and the Staff Manual respectively. Title pages will be prepared in manuscript.

WAR DIARY
or
INTELLIGENCE SUMMARY.
(Erase heading not required.)

Army Form C. 2118.

Place	Date	Hour	Summary of Events and Information	Remarks and references to Appendices
BERNAVILLE	Jul 2		5 cases admitted, includes 3 cases left behind by 18 A.I.S. 29 Div.	
	5		7 admitted.	
	6		9 transferred sick.	
	7		4 admitted, 1 returned to unit cured	
	8		1 admitted, 1 returned to unit cured.	
	9		1 admitted, 1 transferred sick.	
	10		4 admitted.	
	11		1 returned to unit cured	
	12		2 admitted, includes 1 stray from 217 A.S.C.	
	13		1 admitted	
	14		3 admitted, 1 transferred sick. 3 strays collected from Town Major Talmas.	
	15		2 admitted. No TT.02605 Staff Sergt. McKay, R.A.V.C. joined the unit from No 1 Vety Hospital.	
	16		2 admitted. 1 returned to unit cured.	
	17		12 transferred sick. 1 returned to unit cured. 1 L.D. issued to 7th D.C.L.I.	
	18		2 returned to unit cured. 2 mules issued to Hd. Qtrs. 61st Inf. Bde.	
	19		4 admitted, includes 1 stray from 61st Fld Ambulance. 3 transferred sick.	
	20		1 stray admitted from 2nd Cav. Reserve Pk, & handed over to Town Maj. Bernaville	
	21		Unit marched to Doullens, entrained to Godewaersvelde & marched to PROVEN	

A5834 Wt. W4973/M687 750,000 8/16 D. D. & L. Ltd. Forms/C.2118/13.

Instructions regarding War Diaries and Intelligence Summaries are contained in F. S. Regs., Part II. and the Staff Manual respectively. Title pages will be prepared in manuscript.

WAR DIARY
or
INTELLIGENCE SUMMARY.
(Erase heading not required.)

Army Form C. 2118.

Place	Date	Hour	Summary of Events and Information	Remarks and references to Appendices
PROVEN	22		6 admitted 1 returned to unit cured	
	23		9 admitted	
	24		3 admitted 9 transferred sick to XV Corps M.V. Detachment	
	25		5 admitted 5 transferred sick	
	26		6 admitted 2 transferred sick 1 destroyed	
	27		3 admitted 3 transferred sick Moved camp to E18 b 11 Sheet 27	
	28		5 admitted	
	29		3 admitted 25 transferred sick by road to No 23 Vety Hospital St OMER	
	30		1 admitted 1 destroyed	
	31		2 transferred sick to XIV Corps M.V. Detachment	

James [illegible]
Capt AVC
O.C.

32ND MOBILE VETERINARY SECTION, 20TH DIVISION.
No. ......
Date 31.7.17

A5834 Wt. W4973/M687 750,000 8/16 D. D. & L. Ltd. Forms/C.2118/13.

Instructions regarding War Diaries and Intelligence Summaries are contained in F. S. Regs., Part II. and the Staff Manual respectively. Title pages will be prepared in manuscript.

WAR DIARY
or
INTELLIGENCE SUMMARY.
(*Erase heading not required.*)

32 Mob Vety Sec
~~A.V.C.~~
Vol 24

Army Form C. 2118.

Place	Date	Hour	Summary of Events and Information	Remarks and references to Appendices
~~PROVEN~~ E18b11 Sheet 27	Aug 1		1 admitted, 2 transferred sick	
	2		6 admitted	
	3		3 admitted, 4 transferred sick	
	4		2 admitted, 2 transferred sick	
	5		1 transferred sick	
A9c 7/3 Sheet 28	6		1 admitted, 1 destroyed. Unit moved from PROVEN to A9c 7/3, Sheet 28, & put out an advanced post at ELVERDINGHE, B20a53, Sheet 28	
	7		27 admitted, 20 transferred sick, 1 destroyed	
	8		7 admitted, 15 transferred sick	
	9		41 admitted, 25 transferred sick, 1 stray brought in by A/122 Bty. R.F.A. 38th Div. No 6519 Cpl Harris J. A.V.C., reverted to Pte. at own request. No 2241 Pte. Harlow A. F. A.V.C. promoted to L/Cpl.	
	10		18 transferred sick	
	11		21 admitted. 13 transferred sick	
	12		12 admitted, 17 transferred sick	
	13		11 admitted, 10 transferred sick 1 stray brought in by 62nd Fld Amb.	
	14		10 admitted, 2 transferred sick. 2 strays from 20 Div. M. M. P. handed over to 2 Sect. 38th D.A.C. 1 stray brought in by 25th Labour Coy	
	15		10 cases admitted. 17 transferred sick 1 returned to unit cured	

Instructions regarding War Diaries and Intelligence Summaries are contained in F. S. Regs., Part II. and the Staff Manual respectively. Title pages will be prepared in manuscript.

WAR DIARY
or
INTELLIGENCE SUMMARY.

(Erase heading not required.)

Army Form C. 2118.

Place	Date	Hour	Summary of Events and Information	Remarks and references to Appendices
A9c 7.3 Sheet 28	16		54 admitted. 43 transferred sick	
	17		7 admitted 12 transferred sick. 1 strayed into Section's lines. 1 returned to unit cured	
	18		17 admitted, 21 transferred sick	
	19		3 admitted, 2 transferred sick. 2 returned to unit cured. 2 handed over to 49 M.V.S. & unit marched to PROVEN, E18 b 11, Sheet 27	
	20		2 admitted, 2 transferred sick	
	21		11 admitted, 2 transferred sick, 1 returned to unit cured	
	22		8 admitted, 1 returned to unit cured.	
	23		9 admitted, 6 transferred sick. Stray admitted from 158 Coy. A.S.C. & reissued to 60 Coy. A.S.C.	
	24		No 959 Pte Coyle, Thomas admitted to hospital. 16 cases admitted, 2	
	25		1 animal reissued to 11 R.B.	
	27		5 cases admitted, 5 transferred sick, 1 returned to unit cured.	
	29		3 admitted, 4 transferred sick. 1 reissued to 10 R.B., 2 to 20th Div. Hd. Qrs.	32ND MOBILE VETERINARY SECTION. 20TH DIVISION. No. .... Date ....
	30		8 admitted	
	31		8 transferred sick.	

[illegible] Capt. A.V.C.
O.C.

A5834 Wt. W4973/M687 750,000 8/16 D. D. & L. Ltd. Forms/C.2118/13.

Vol 25

WAR DIARY

32nd Mobile Vet. Section

Sept 1917

Instructions regarding War Diaries and Intelligence Summaries are contained in F. S. Regs., Part II. and the Staff Manual respectively. Title pages will be prepared in manuscript.

WAR DIARY
or
INTELLIGENCE SUMMARY.
(Erase heading not required.)

Army Form C. 2118.

82ND MOBILE VETERINARY SECTION. 20TH DIVISION.
No..........
Date..........

Place	Date	Hour	Summary of Events and Information	Remarks and references to Appendices
E18 b 11 Sheet 27	Sept 1		2 cases admitted, 11 transferred sick 8 returned to unit cured	
	2		1 admitted 2 transferred sick	
	3		1 admitted 2 returned to unit cured & 1 destroyed.	
	4		2 transferred sick	
	5		1 admitted	
	6		1 admitted	
	7		2 admitted, 2 transferred sick	
	8		2 transferred sick.	
	9		2 admitted, 2 transferred sick	
	10		5 cases admitted, 5 transferred sick	
A9c73 Sheet 28	11		10 admitted. Unit moved to A 9 c 7 3 Sheet 28 & took over an advanced Veterinary Collecting Post at B 20 a 5 3 Sheet 28	
	12		22 cases admitted. 20 transferred sick. 1 to A.R.D. No 2241 Cpl. Harlow A.J. admitted to Hospital (18 C.C.S.)	
	13		19 admitted 27 transferred sick	
	14		19 admitted 15 transferred sick. 1 returned to unit cured No 8577 Pte Green A.J. joined from No 2 Vety. Hospital	
	15		14 admitted 22 transferred sick, 1 died	

A5834 Wt. W4973/M687 750,000 8/16 D. D. & L. Ltd. Forms/C.2118/13.

Instructions regarding War Diaries and Intelligence Summaries are contained in F. S. Regs., Part II. and the Staff Manual respectively. Title pages will be prepared in manuscript.

WAR DIARY
or
INTELLIGENCE SUMMARY.
(Erase heading not required.)

Army Form C. 2118.

Place	Date	Hour	Summary of Events and Information	Remarks and references to Appendices
A9c 7 3 Sheet 28	16		3 admitted 1 transferred sick.	
	17		14 admitted. 16 transferred sick.	
	18		20 admitted 20 transferred sick	
	19		16 admitted 8 transferred sick, 1 destroyed.	
	20		5 admitted. ~~Pte~~ No 1734 Pte. Newman A. admitted to hospital.	
	21		33 admitted 38 transferred sick	
	22		19 admitted. 15 transferred sick	
	23		6 admitted 15 transferred sick	
	24		9 admitted.	
	25		16 admitted. 42 transferred sick.	
	26		6 admitted. 7 transferred sick	
	27		6 admitted. ~~Pte Rejo~~ No 970 Pte. Kendall A.G. joined from No 2 Vety. Hospital	
	28		3 admitted, 14 transferred sick & 1 destroyed.	
	29		6 cases & 2 strays admitted. 8 transferred sick. Unit moved to PROVEN Sheet 27 E18 b11.	
	30		2 cases transferred sick.	

32ND MOBILE VETERINARY SECTION, 20TH DIVISION.
No.............
Date...........

[signature] Capt. A.V.C.
6.C.

A5834 Wt. W4973/M687 750,000 8/16 D. D. & L. Ltd. Forms/C.2118/13.

Instructions regarding War Diaries and Intelligence Summaries are contained in F. S. Regs., Part II. and the Staff Manual respectively. Title pages will be prepared in manuscript.

35th M.V.S

WAR DIARY
or
INTELLIGENCE SUMMARY.
~~H.Q.~~ Mob Vety Sec

(*Erase heading not required.*)

Army Form C. 2118.

Vol 26

Place	Date	Hour	Summary of Events and Information	Remarks and references to Appendices
[illegible]	Oct 1		Unit marched to HOPOUTRE & entrained from there to BAPAUME	
	2		Unit marched to LE MESNIL and took over billet of 4th West Lancs Mob Vety Sec 55th Div	
	3		1 case admitted.	
	4		No 1675 Pte Guy J reported to the unit for duty from No 2 Vety Hospital	
	5		1 case destroyed	
	6		Unit marched to MOISLAINS & took over billet of 51st Mob Vety Sec 40th Div	
	8		No 6526 Cpl. Briggs P.G. despatched to No 2 Vety Hospital. Took over advanced collecting post at NURLU. Lorry [illegible]	
	9		1 Cpl. 3 men despatched to 3rd Corps Mob. Vety Detachment	
	10		6 cases admitted	
	11		2 cases admitted	
	12		No 26723 Pte BACKELL G.H. reported to the unit from No 4 Vety Hospital. Collecting [illegible] moved from NURLU to FINS	
	13		1 animal destroyed	
	14		6 admitted 1 destroyed 1 stray mule brought in by 20 Div M.M.P. 6 C[illegible] on [illegible]	
	15		6 cases admitted	

A5834 Wt. W4973/M687 750,000 8/16 D. D. & L. Ltd. Forms/C.2118/13.

Instructions regarding War Diaries and Intelligence Summaries are contained in F. S. Regs., Part II. and the Staff Manual respectively. Title pages will be prepared in manuscript.

WAR DIARY
or
INTELLIGENCE SUMMARY.
(Erase heading not required.)

Army Form C. 2118.

Place	Date	Hour	Summary of Events and Information	Remarks and references to Appendices
MOISLAINS	16		1 admitted 10 transferred sick	
	19		6 admitted	
	20		3 admitted 7 transferred sick	
	21		1 admitted 1 died 1 stray brought in by 57 M.G.C. (mule)	
	22		6 admitted	
	23		1 admitted 7 transferred sick	
	24		3 admitted	
	25		1 admitted	
	26		2 admitted	
	27		5 admitted 4 transferred sick. 1 stray mule issued to 61st Bde. Hd. Qrs.	
	29		4 admitted	
	30		4 transferred sick. 1 stray mule issued to 21/ M.G.C.	
	31		2 admitted 1 mule issued to 84th Fd. Coy R.E.	

[illegible signature]
Capt. C.O.

A5834 Wt. W4973/M687 750,000 8/16 D. D. & L. Ltd. Forms/C.2118/13.

Instructions regarding War Diaries and Intelligence Summaries are contained in F. S. Regs., Part II. and the Staff Manual respectively. Title pages will be prepared in manuscript.

WAR DIARY
or
INTELLIGENCE SUMMARY.
(Erase heading not required.)

Army Form C. 2118.

32 Mob Vety Sec
Vol 27

Place	Date	Hour	Summary of Events and Information	Remarks and references to Appendices
MOISLAINS	Nov 1		1 case admitted 1 NCO. & 3 men returned from 3rd Corps. M.V.D	
	2		13 admitted. 1 stray horse brought in by M.M.P.	
	3		4 admitted, 12 transferred sick.	
	5		12 admitted, 1 mule returned to 83rd Fld Coy. R.E	
	6		1 admitted, 16 transferred sick	
	7		2 admitted	
	8		5 admitted	
	9		1 admitted, 6 transferred sick	
	10		3 admitted, 1 destroyed.	
	11		6 admitted, 6026 Cpl. Biggs A.V.C. invalided to England	
	12		5 admitted	
	13		1 admitted 5 transferred sick, 1 destroyed	
	14		4 admitted, 1 destroyed	
	15		8 admitted	
	16		1 admitted 22 transferred sick	
	17		12 admitted. Advanced post moved to SOREL	

Instructions regarding War Diaries and Intelligence Summaries are contained in F. S. Regs., Part II. and the Staff Manual respectively. Title pages will be prepared in manuscript.

WAR DIARY
or
INTELLIGENCE SUMMARY.
(Erase heading not required.)

Army Form C. 2118.

Place	Date	Hour	Summary of Events and Information	Remarks and references to Appendices
MOISLAINS	18		6 cases admitted	
	19		2 admitted	
	20		4 admitted, 40 evacuated sick 1 stray mule brought in by 62nd [illegible] Aust. Issued & returned to unit	
	21		1 admitted. Advanced post moved to GOUZEACOURT	
	22		1 admitted. 4 evacuated sick 3 stray riders brought in by 20 Div M.M.P. Section moved to GOUZEACOURT W4a58 Sheet 57c.	
GOUZEACOURT	23		3 admitted 10 evacuated sick 1 horse issued to 84th [illegible]	
	24		2 admitted 2 evacuated sick	
	25		4 admitted. 4 evacuated sick. 1 returned to unit cured	
	26		1 admitted	
	27		1 admitted 4 evacuated sick	
	28		4 admitted 2 died Unit moved to NURLU D4a91 Sheet 62c.	
	29		1 admitted 5 evacuated sick 1 stray mule brought in by 20 Div M.M.P. Section marched to MOISLAINS C12c88. Sheet 62c	

[illegible signature] Capt. A.V.C. [illegible]

32ND MOBILE VETERINARY SECTION 20TH DIVISION.

A5834 Wt. W4973/M687 750,000 8/16 D. D. & L. Ltd. Forms/C.2118/13.

Instructions regarding War Diaries and Intelligence Summaries are contained in F. S. Regs., Part II. and the Staff Manual respectively. Title pages will be prepared in manuscript.

WAR DIARY
or
INTELLIGENCE SUMMARY.
(*Erase heading not required.*)

32nd M.V.S.

Vol 28

Army Form C. 2118.

Place	Date	Hour	Summary of Events and Information	Remarks and references to Appendices
	Dec 1917			
MOISLAINS	1		13 cases admitted.	
	2		7 admitted. 11 transferred sick	
	3		15 admitted 14 transferred sick. 1 stray horse L.D. brought in by D/92 Bde. R.F.A.	
	4		10 transferred sick. Unit marched to MEAULTE.	
MEAULTE	5		Unit marched to AMPLIER	
AMPLIER	6		Unit marched to PETIT FILLIEVRES.	
PETIT FILLIEVRES	7		Unit marched to MARCONNELLE.	
MARCONNELLE	8		Unit marched to WAILLY.	
WAILLY	10		1 case admitted	
	11		2 cases admitted & 6 collected from civilians. No 26723 Pte BACHELL, G.H. invalided to England.	
RACQUINGHEM	12		7 transferred sick. Unit marched to RACQUINGHEM	
	16		4 admitted	
	17		1 transferred sick 1 cured & returned to duty (Father Scully's)	
	18		5 admitted.	
	19		1 admitted. 10 transferred sick.	

A5834 Wt. W4973/M687 750,000 8/16 D. D. & L. Ltd. Forms/C.2118/13.

Instructions regarding War Diaries and Intelligence Summaries are contained in F. S. Regs., Part II. and the Staff Manual respectively. Title pages will be prepared in manuscript.

WAR DIARY
or
INTELLIGENCE SUMMARY.
(Erase heading not required.)

Army Form C. 2118.

Place	Date	Hour	Summary of Events and Information	Remarks and references to Appendices
RACQUINGHEM	20		3 admitted. 1 stray mule brought in by 20 M.M.P.	
	21		10 men arrived from No 4 Vety Hospital Base viz No SE 23643 Pte Bocking A.F, No S.E 15285 Pte Bocking C.A., No S.E 15208 Pte HOLT J., No S.E 9438 Pte JARMAN E, No S.E 20646 Pte HAYES, W. No S.E. 21632 Pte BARKER A. No S.E. 30454 Pte HINGLEY J. No S.R 54 Pte BOWER J. No TT 03409 Pte WYATT. A., No S.E 27015 Pte POTTER F.	
	22		3 transferred sick. 9 men despatched to No 2 Vety Hospital viz No 6419 Pte BUTTERWORTH J.W No 11808 PTE COWAN A., No 4492 Pte HARVEY F, No 564 Pte KNIGHT J. No 11085 Pte LAWSON F, No 1399 PTE RAWLINGS E. No 6743 Pte MOSS H, No 3643 Pte SAUNDERS J, & No 1504 Pte WAITE E.	
	23		1 stray riders brought in from 11 KRR	
	24		4 admitted.	
	26		1 admitted. 1 stray rider brought in by 20 M.M.P. DADVS's charger destroyed. SR 54	
	27		Pte BOWER J & SE 27015 Pte POTTER F invalided to C.C.S.	
	28		No 24542 Pte SMITH C. reported from No 2 Vety Hospital for duty	
	29		1 stray mule issued to 61st Fd. Ambulance.	

17

Instructions regarding War Diaries and Intelligence Summaries are contained in F. S. Regs., Part II. and the Staff Manual respectively. Title pages will be prepared in manuscript.

WAR DIARY
or
INTELLIGENCE SUMMARY.
(Erase heading not required.)

Army Form C. 2118.

32nd Mob. Vet Section

Vol 29

Place	Date	Hour	Summary of Events and Information	Remarks and references to Appendices
RACQUINGHEM	Jan 3		Pte HINGLEY J. admitted to 61st Fd. Ambulance.	
	4		Unit marched to METEREN	
METEREN	6		1 case admitted. Unit marched to WESTOUTRE map reference Sheet 28 – M 2 d 8 0. No 30754 Pte HINGLEY J. AVC. transferred to IX Corps Rest Station	
WESTOUTRE	7		2 cases admitted	
	8		13 admitted. No 20646 Pte HAYES. W, No 18208 Pte HOLT. J, No 27542 Pte SMITH, C, & No TT 0309 Pte WYATT A temporarily detached to IX Corps V.C.C.S.	
	9		15 cases admitted. Cpl. CROWE. C.R. evacuated to C.C.S.	
	10		5 admitted. 15 transferred sick.	
	11		No 3983 Pte TODD G, & No 848 Pte TIERNEY W joined the unit from No 2 Vety Hospital	
	12		No T/1/3871 Dr MIZEN. W. ASC admitted 61st Fd. Ambulance	
	14		7 cases admitted. 6 transferred sick.	
	15		13 cases admitted	
	16		2 cases admitted	
	17		3 cases admitted 28 transferred sick.	

A5834 Wt. W4973/M687 750,000 8/16 D. D. & L. Ltd. Forms/C.2118/13.

Instructions regarding War Diaries and Intelligence Summaries are contained in F. S. Regs., Part II. and the Staff Manual respectively. Title pages will be prepared in manuscript.

WAR DIARY
or
INTELLIGENCE SUMMARY.
(Erase heading not required.)

Army Form C. 2118.

Place	Date	Hour	Summary of Events and Information	Remarks and references to Appendices
WESTOUTRE	18		5 cases admitted	
	19		4 admitted 3 transferred sick to L of C	
	21		10 admitted 1 transferred sick, 1 destroyed.	
	22		9 admitted.	
	24		32 transferred sick. No 6453 L/Cpl ROSE, T. & No 6743 Pte MOSS H rejoined the unit from No 2 Vety. Hospital	
	25		No 30754 Pte HINGLEY J, surplus to establishment, sent to No 2 Vety. Hospital 6 cases admitted	
	26		8 cases admitted.	
	28		8 cases admitted.	
	30		2 admitted	
	31		3 admitted 33 transferred sick. Pte POTTER F AVC, surplus to establishment, sent to 2 Vety Hospital No 970 Pte KENDALL A G AVC struck off strength on admittance to NETLEY HOSPITAL England	

James B. Wildham
Capt AVC (T.C.)
6 C.

A5834 Wt. W4973/M687 750,000 8/16 D. D. & L. Ltd. Forms/C.2118/13.

14

Instructions regarding War Diaries and Intelligence Summaries are contained in F. S. Regs., Part II. and the Staff Manual respectively. Title pages will be prepared in manuscript.

WAR DIARY
or
INTELLIGENCE SUMMARY.
(Erase heading not required.)

Army Form C. 2118.

32 Mob Vety Sec
20 D
Vol 30

Place	Date	Hour	Summary of Events and Information	Remarks and references to Appendices
WESTOUTRE	26.1		3 cases admitted	
	2		4 admitted	
	3		11 admitted Pte ESDALE E.C. joined the unit	
	4		13 admitted 9 transferred sick	
	5		Pte GREEN H. left the unit for No 2 Vety Hospital HAVRE. 26 cases admitted	
	6		2 admitted	
	7		28 transferred sick 2 admitted	
	8		5 admitted	
	9		5 admitted	
	10		2 admitted	
	11		6 transferred sick No 7553 Pte BROMLEY H joined the unit from No 2 Vety Hospital HAVRE	
	12		11 admitted	
	13		6 admitted	
	14		1 admitted 19 transferred sick	

A5834. Wt. W4973/M687 750,000 8/16 D. D. & L. Ltd. Forms/C.2118/13.

Instructions regarding War Diaries and Intelligence Summaries are contained in F. S. Regs., Part II. and the Staff Manual respectively. Title pages will be prepared in manuscript.

WAR DIARY
or
INTELLIGENCE SUMMARY.
(Erase heading not required.)

Army Form C. 2118.

Place	Date	Hour	Summary of Events and Information	Remarks and references to Appendices
WESTOUTRE	15 [illegible]		1 case admitted	
PRADELLES	16		Unit marched to PRADELLES	
RACQUINGHEM	17		" " " RACQUINGHEM	
	18		3 cases admitted	
	19		9 " "	
	20		2 " "	
	21		1 " " 16 transferred evac.	
	22		transferred evac. Unit marched to STEENBECQUE	
	23		Entrained at STEENBECQUE at 10 a.m. & proceeded to NESLE, arriving 2 p.m. detrained & marched to ~~[illegible]~~ ERCHEUX	
ERCHEUX	24		2 cases admitted	
	25		3 " "	
	26		3 " "	
	27		1 " "	
	28		6 " "	

James B. Wallace
Capt. A.V.C.
O.C.

A5834 Wt. W4973/M687 750,000 8/16 D. D. & L. Ltd. Forms/C.2118/13.

Instructions regarding War Diaries and Intelligence Summaries are contained in F. S. Regs., Part II. and the Staff Manual respectively. Title pages will be prepared in manuscript.

WAR DIARY
or
INTELLIGENCE SUMMARY.
(Erase heading not required.)

Army Form C. 2118.

Place	Date	Hour	Summary of Events and Information	Remarks and references to Appendices
ERCHEU	Mar 5		18 cases transferred sick to L. of C. 1 destroyed.	
	6		1 admitted ~~destroyed~~	
	7		0 admitted.	
	8		3 admitted.	
	9		1 admitted.	
	10		2 admitted.	
	11		6 admitted.	
	12		2 admitted, 22 transferred sick.	
	13		1 admitted.	
	14		2 admitted	
	15		2 admitted	
	16		2 admitted	
	17		4 admitted	
	18		7 admitted	
	19		18 transferred sick.	

A5834 Wt. W4973/M687 750,000 8/16 D. D. & L. Ltd. Forms/C.2118/13.

Army Form C. 2118.

32nd M.V.S. 20 D

Vol 31

WAR DIARY
or
INTELLIGENCE SUMMARY.
(Erase heading not required.)

Instructions regarding War Diaries and Intelligence Summaries are contained in F. S. Regs., Part II. and the Staff Manual respectively. Title pages will be prepared in manuscript.

Place	Date	Hour	Summary of Events and Information	Remarks and references to Appendices
ERCHEU	20		1 case admitted.	
	21		Unit marched to St SULPICE	
	22		5 admitted from 40 M.V.S. 2 destroyed. Unit moved to OFFEY	
	23		Unit moved to ESMERY HALLON, ERCHEU & ROYE.	
	24		Unit moved to CARREPUITS, took over 1 stray mule, 2 cases admitted, 1 destroyed	
	25		Unit moved to HANGEST 1 admitted, 1 destroyed. Unit moved to MOREUIL	
	26		2 cases admitted.	
	27		3 admitted Unit marched to DOMART SUR LA LUCE	
	28		3 admitted Unit marched to BOVES.	
	29		3 admitted	
	30		3 admitted. 2 destroyed. Unit moved to SAINS EN AMIENOIS	
	31		4 admitted 19 transferred sick to 20th V.C.C.S. PICQUIGNY	

James Oldham Capt. A.V.C.

A5834 Wt. W4973/M687 750,000 8/16 D. D. & L. Ltd. Forms/C.2118/13.

7

Instructions regarding War Diaries and Intelligence Summaries are contained in F. S. Regs., Part II. and the Staff Manual respectively. Title pages will be prepared in manuscript.

April

WAR DIARY
or
INTELLIGENCE SUMMARY.
(Erase heading not required.)

Army Form C. 2118.

32 Mob. Vety Sec

20

Vol 32

Place	Date	Hour	Summary of Events and Information	Remarks and references to Appendices
SAINS EN AMIENOIS	1		19 cases admitted. 13 transferred sick 1 destroyed	
	2		8 admitted 16 transferred sick	
	3		27 admitted. 14 transferred sick	
	4		30 admitted 29 transferred sick 1 destroyed.	
	5		19 admitted 22 transferred sick. 2 destroyed	
	6		4 admitted. Unit moved to DURY	
	7		9 admitted	
	8		10 transferred sick. Unit moved to LINCHEUX.	
	10		Unit moved to GREBAULT.	
	11		Unit moved to CAMACHES. 2 cases admitted	
	12		2 transferred sick	
	13		1 admitted. [illegible] T4036724 Dr Hubbard joined the unit from 158 Coy. ASC	
	14		Unit moved to BAZINVAL 5 cases admitted. 2 transferred sick	
	15		Unit moved to BUIGNY 2 cases admitted.	

A5834 Wt. W4973/M687 750,000 8/16 D. D. & L. Ltd. Forms/C.2118/13.

Instructions regarding War Diaries and Intelligence Summaries are contained in F. S. Regs., Part II. and the Staff Manual respectively. Title pages will be prepared in manuscript.

WAR DIARY
or
INTELLIGENCE SUMMARY.
(*Erase heading not required.*)

Army Form C. 2118.

April

Place	Date	Hour	Summary of Events and Information	Remarks and references to Appendices
BUIGNY	16		2 cases admitted. 4 transferred sick	
	17		Unit moved to EPAGNE 3 cases admitted	
	18		Unit marched to FROHEN LE GRAND	
	19		Unit marched to TOUFFLIN RICAMETZ	
	20		Unit marched to MINGOVAL	
	21		1 case admitted. No 6743 Pte MOSS H. & 21632 Pte BARKER A. A.V.C. despatched to No 2 Vety Hospital, HAVRE for training as Sergts. A.V.C. to Field Units.	
	22		6 cases admitted.	
	23		5 admitted.	
	24		1 admitted. 12 transferred sick.	
	26		2 admitted. 1 died.	
	27		1 destroyed	
	28		2 admitted.	
	30		No 17699 Pte ROBINS J. & 21806 Pte KENTCH H. A.V.C. joined from No [illegible] Vety Hospital	

32ND MOBILE VETERINARY SECTION, 20TH DIVISION.
No.........
Date.........

G B BEVILLE

James B Whitham Capt. A.V.C. O.C.

A5834 Wt. W4973/M687 750,000 8/16 D. D. & L. Ltd. Forms/C.2118/13.

Instructions regarding War Diaries and Intelligence Summaries are contained in F. S. Regs., Part II. and the Staff Manual respectively. Title pages will be prepared in manuscript.

19 May.

WAR DIARY
or
INTELLIGENCE SUMMARY
(Erase heading not required.)

32 Mob Vet Section

Vol 33

Army Form C. 2118.

20

Place	Date	Hour	Summary of Events and Information	Remarks and references to Appendices
MINGOVAL	1		6 Cases transferred 1 case admitted.	
	2		Section left Mingoval & marched to VILLERS au BOIS.	
	3		2 cases admitted.	
	4		1 case admitted	
	5		Section left Villers au Bois & marched to PETIT SERVINS.	
	6		30 cases admitted.	
	7		24 cases transferred. 21 cases admitted.	
	8		29 cases transferred. 9 cases admitted.	
	9		3 cases admitted.	
	10		13 cases transferred. 3 cases admitted.	
	11		12 cases admitted.	
	12		4 cases admitted 13 cases transferred.	
	13		3 cases admitted.	
	14		14 Cases admitted Capt. P.T. Lindsay A.V.C. (S.R.) reported to take charge of Section.	
	15		20 Cases Transferred 8 cases admitted.	
	16		1 case admitted.	
	17		8 Cases Transferred. Capt. D.B. Welham transferred to 13th Corps. also No. 27542 Pte Nash A.J.	
			2 cases admitted.	
	18		6 cases admitted.	
	19		1 case admitted. 6 Men transferred to XVIII th Corps. V.E.S.	
	20		6 Cases transferred. 8 admitted.	
	21		10 Cases transferred 10 admitted.	
	22		5 Cases transferred 13 admitted.	
	23		12 Cases transferred 2 cases admitted.	

A5834 Wt. W4973/M687 750,000 8/16 D. D. & L. Ltd. Forms/C.2118/13.

Instructions regarding War Diaries and Intelligence Summaries are contained in F. S. Regs., Part II. and the Staff Manual respectively. Title pages will be prepared in manuscript.

May.

WAR DIARY
or
INTELLIGENCE SUMMARY.
(Erase heading not required.)

Army Form C. 2118.

Place	Date	Hour	Summary of Events and Information	Remarks and references to Appendices
PETIT. SERVINS	24		3 Cases Admitted.	
	25		7 cases Transferred 9 cases Admitted.	
	26		3 cases Admitted.	
	27		13 cases Transferred 9 cases Admitted.	
	28		8 cases Admitted.	
	29		16 cases Transferred 10 cases Admitted.	
	30		9 cases Transferred 11 cases Admitted.	
	31		7 cases Admitted	

32ND MOBILE VETERINARY SECTION, 50TH DIVISION.
No. ....
Date 31/5/16

R. Lindsay Capt. A.V.C.

A5834 Wt. W4973/M687 750,000 8/16 D. D. & L. Ltd. Forms/C.2118/13.

14

Instructions regarding War Diaries and Intelligence Summaries are contained in F. S. Regs., Part II. and the Staff Manual respectively. Title pages will be prepared in manuscript.

June.

WAR DIARY
or
INTELLIGENCE SUMMARY.
(Erase heading not required.)

Army Form C. 2118.

32 Mob Vety ~~No~~ Section

9/8 28

20

Place	Date	Hour	Summary of Events and Information	Remarks and references to Appendices
Petit Sermin	1.		13 cases admitted. 14 cases transferred.	
	2		2 cases admitted. 14 cases transferred. 156645 Pte Lee A. returned to 221 Employment Coy. T.T. 02605 S/Sgt. McKay proceeded as Senior N.C.O. to XVIIIth. Corps. V.E.S.	
	3.		4 cases Admitted. 2 cases sold to Butcher. 142461 Pte. McKeown joined section for temporary duty from 20th Salvage Coy.	
	4.		9 cases Admitted. 1 case transferred.	
	5.		8 cases Admitted. 14 cases transferred.	
	6		4 cases Admitted. Sergt. McGuinness W.E. proceeded to England on special leave, 14 days.	
	7.		3 cases admitted. 8 cases transferred.	
	8.		6 Cases Admitted	
	9.		1 Case Admitted. 8 cases transferred. 2 cases sold to Butcher.	
	10.		5 Cases Admitted. 142461 Pte McKeown reported at 60th Field Ambulance to be medically examined	
	11.		2 cases admitted.	
	12.		5 Cases Admitted. 9 cases transferred.	
	13		5 Cases Admitted.	
	14		5 Cases Admitted.	

82nd MOBILE VETERINARY SECTION. 20TH DIVISION. No. ...... Date 30.6.18

A5834 Wt. W4973/M687 750,000 8/16 D. D. & L. Ltd. Forms/C.2118/13.

Army Form C. 2118.

Instructions regarding War Diaries and Intelligence Summaries are contained in F. S. Regs., Part II. and the Staff Manual respectively. Title pages will be prepared in manuscript.

June

WAR DIARY
or
INTELLIGENCE SUMMARY.
(*Erase heading not required.*)

Place	Date	Hour	Summary of Events and Information	Remarks and references to Appendices
Petit Servins	15.		12 Cases admitted. 12 cases transferred.	
	16		8 Cases Admitted 12 cases transferred.	
	17		Nothing to Report.	
	18.		2 cases admitted. 8 cases transferred.	
	19		Nothing to Report.	
	20		4 cases Admitted	
	21		5 Cases Admitted. 22225 Pte. Clarke A. J. joined this section from No. 2 Vety. Hospital.	
	22		10 Cases transferred. 23643 Pte Borking A. F. admitted to 60th Field Ambulance	
	23.		9 cases Admitted. 83882 Pte. Watts, F.W. joined this section for temporary duty from ~~221 Emp~~ P.P.L 20th Salvage Coy.	
	24.		10 cases transferred.	
	25.		T/31533 Dr. Brown A. 3131 Pte. Jelly R.K., 15285 Pte. Borking C.A. admitted to 60th Field Ambulance. 1 Animal sold to Butcher.	
	26.		27542 Pte. Smith C., 6727 Pte. Knight A.; T/4/036724 Dr. Hubbard G. admitted to 60th Field Ambulance. 6 cases admitted to Section.	82ND MOBILE VETERINARY SECTION. 20TH DIVISION. No. — Date 30 6 18

Army Form C. 2118.

WAR DIARY
or
INTELLIGENCE SUMMARY.
(*Erase heading not required.*)

Instructions regarding War Diaries and Intelligence Summaries are contained in F. S. Regs., Part II. and the Staff Manual respectively. Title pages will be prepared in manuscript.

June

Place	Date	Hour	Summary of Events and Information	Remarks and references to Appendices
Petit Servins	27		5 cases admitted. 9 cases transferred. Sergt. McGuinness returned from leave.	
	28		8 cases admitted. 15285 Pte. Bocking C.A.; 3131 Pte. Filby R.K. returned to duty. 6519 a/Cpl. Harris J.W.; 6752 Pte. Davies W.H.; 9738 Pte Jarman E.; 200846 a/Cpl. Read A.J. admitted to 60th Field Ambulance.	
	29		3 cases admitted. 14 cases transferred: 23643 Pte. Bocking A.J. returned to duty.	
	30		2 cases admitted, & one stray horse handed in by No. 2 Sect. D.A.C. 27542 Pte. Smith C. returned to duty.	

P. T. Lindsay Capt. A.V.C.

82ND MOBILE VETERINARY SECTION, 20TH DIVISION.
No. —
Date 30. 6. 18

A5834 Wt. W4973/M687 750,000 8/16 D. D. & L. Ltd. Forms/C.2118/13.

11

Instructions regarding War Diaries and Intelligence Summaries are contained in F. S. Regs., Part II. and the Staff Manual respectively. Title pages will be prepared in manuscript.

WAR DIARY
or
INTELLIGENCE SUMMARY.
(Erase heading not required.)

Army Form C. 2118.

32 Mob Vety Sec
July.
Vol 35

20

Place	Date	Hour	Summary of Events and Information	Remarks and references to Appendices
Petit Sowin	July 1		4 Cases Admitted, 1 case transferred. 6727 Pte. Knight A. returned to duty. 1 Stray Horse claimed by a/48 Army Bde. R.F.A.	
	2		7 Cases admitted. T/31533 Dr. Brown A returned to duty.	
	3.		8 cases Admitted. 5 cases transferred. 6519 a/Cpl. Harris J.W. 200846 a/Cpl. Read A.J., 9738 Pte. Jarman E. returned to duty.	
	4		2 cases Admitted. 7 cases transferred.	
	5		2 Cases admitted.	
	6		10 Cases Admitted. 5 Cases transferred. 1 Stray admitted. T/4/036724 Dr. Hubbard G. returned to duty.	
	7		3 cases Admitted. 10 cases transferred.	
	8		7 Cases Admitted. 1 cases Butchered.	
	9		3 Cases admitted. 7 cases transferred, 2 cases butchered.	
	10		6 Cases Admitted, 7 Cases transferred.	
	11		7 Cases transferred	
	12		1 Case Admitted.	
	13		4 Cases Admitted. 22542 Pte. Smith C. proceeded on leave to England.	
	14.		5 cases transferred	
	15.		4 Cases Admitted. 1 case Butchered	
	16.		5 Cases Admitted. 1 Case Died. 2 cases cured & returned to unit.	

Army Form C. 2118.

Instructions regarding War Diaries and Intelligence Summaries are contained in F. S. Regs., Part II. and the Staff Manual respectively. Title pages will be prepared in manuscript.

WAR DIARY
or
INTELLIGENCE SUMMARY.
(Erase heading not required.)

July

Place	Date	Hour	Summary of Events and Information	Remarks and references to Appendices
Petit Servins	July 17		7 cases transferred	
	18		1 case Admitted.	
	19		2 cases Admitted,	
	20		1 Case Admitted.	
	21		5 cases Admitted,	
	22		2 Cases Admitted, 9 cases transferred,	
	23		3 Cases Admitted.	
	24		6 Cases Admitted,	
	25		5 Cases Admitted, 9 cases transferred	
	26		14 Cases Admitted. 1 case transferred, 1 butchered, 1 Destroyed, (tetanus)	
	27		9 Cases Admitted. 14 cases transferred,	
	28		4 Cases Admitted. 7 cases transferred	
	29		6 Cases Admitted. 1 Case transferred, 1 case Butchered,	
	30		5 cases Admitted. 2 cases transferred 27542 Pte Smith C. returned from leave.	
	31		1 case Admitted 8 cases transferred	

P. T. Lindsay Capt. AVC

13

Instructions regarding War Diaries and Intelligence Summaries are contained in F. S. Regs., Part II. and the Staff Manual respectively. Title pages will be prepared in manuscript.

WAR DIARY
or
INTELLIGENCE SUMMARY.
(Erase heading not required.)

32 Mobile Vety Sec
August.

Army Form C. 2118.

20

Vol 36

Place	Date	Hour	Summary of Events and Information	Remarks and references to Appendices
Petit Sévins	1/8/18		5 cases admitted 5 cases transferred	
	2/8/18		5 cases admitted.	
	3/8/18		5 cases admitted. 9 cases transferred	
	4/8/18		Nil.	
	5/8/18		4 cases admitted.	
	6/8/18		13 cases admitted	
	7/8/18		1 case admitted. 10 cases transferred.	
	8/8/18		3 cases admitted.	
	9/8/18		4 cases admitted.	
	10/8/18		1 cases admitted. 9 cases transferred.	
	11/8/18		1 stray admitted.	
	12/8/18		3 cases admitted. 1 stray claimed by 20th D.A.C.	
	13/8/18		4 cases admitted. 1 case transferred.	
			No. 2379 Pte. Skinner F. } Reported for duty in Section.	
			" 6544 Pte. Perry G.R. }	
			" 19756 Pte. Stevinson W. }	
	14/8/18		6 cases admitted. 5 cases transferred	
	15/8/18		6 cases admitted. 6 cases transferred. 1 case Butchered.	
	16/8/18		2 cases admitted. 7 cases transferred	
	17/8/18		1 case admitted. 1 case died. No. 3131 Pte Digby R.K. admitted to 60 Fd. Ambulance.	
			No. 1075 Cpl. Guy J. } Proceeded to No. 2 Vety. Hospital for Medical Examination	
			" 9667 Cpl. Morgan K. }	
	18/8/18		1 case admitted. No. 23643 Pte. Booking A.7. admitted to 60th Field Ambulance.	
	19/8/18		4 cases admitted.	

82ND MOBILE VETERINARY SECTION, 20TH DIVISION.
No.
Date

A5834 Wt. W4973/M687 750,000 8/16 D. D. & L. Ltd. Forms/C.2118/13.

Instructions regarding War Diaries and Intelligence Summaries are contained in F. S. Regs., Part II. and the Staff Manual respectively. Title pages will be prepared in manuscript.

WAR DIARY
or
INTELLIGENCE SUMMARY.
(Erase heading not required.)

Army Form C. 2118.

August.

Place	Date	Hour	Summary of Events and Information	Remarks and references to Appendices
Petit Servins	20/8/18.		1 Case Cured.	
	21/8/18		1 Case admitted. 6 cases transferred.	
	22/8/18		3 cases admitted.	
	23/8/18		8 cases admitted. No. 1075 Cpl. Guy G. / " 9667 Cpl. Morgan R. } Return from No. 2 Vety. Hospital	
	24/8/18		2 cases admitted. 11 cases transferred.	
	25/8/18		1 case admitted.	
	26/8/18		11 cases admitted. 2 Horses admitted from 20th D.A.C. (Remounts) awaiting Re-issue	
	27/8/18		5 cases admitted. 4 cases transferred	
	28/8/18		3 cases admitted. 15 cases transferred; No. 1079 Pte. McTiernan J, reported for duty in Section from No. 2 Vety. Hospital	
	29/8/18		1 case admitted. 1 Stray admitted.	
	30/8/18.		1 case admitted. 2 Horses. (Remounts) reissued to B.92 Bde. R.F.A.	
	31/8/18.		1 Case admitted.	

P. Lindsay Capt. A.V.C.

32ND MOBILE VETERINARY SECTION, 20TH DIVISION.
No.
Date

A5834 Wt. W4973/M687 750,000 8/16 D. D. & L. Ltd. Forms/C.2118/13.

14 20

Instructions regarding War Diaries and Intelligence Summaries are contained in F. S. Regs., Part II. and the Staff Manual respectively. Title pages will be prepared in manuscript.

WAR DIARY
or
INTELLIGENCE SUMMARY.
(Erase heading not required.)

Army Form C. 2118.

32 Mob Vety Sec

September

WO 37

Place	Date	Hour	Summary of Events and Information	Remarks and references to Appendices
PETIT SERVINS	1/9/18		Six cases admitted. 8 transferred.	
	2/9/18		5 Cases Admitted 5 Cases transferred, 1 Case Butchered;	
	3/9/18		6 Cases Admitted. No. T/4/036724 Dr. Hubbard admitted to 60th Field Ambulance.	
	4/9/18		2 cases Admitted. 11 Cases transferred No. 3131 Pte. Tilly R.R. discharged from Hospital.	
	5/9/18		No3131 Pte Tilly R.R. proceeded to No. Vety. Hospital for medical examination. No 15285 Pte. Booking C.A. proceeded on leave to England. 1 case admitted.	
	6/9/18		4 Cases Admitted.	
	7/9/18		7 Cases Admitted.	
	8/9/18		5 Cases Admitted.	
	9/9/18		3 Cases Admitted. 11 Cases transferred.	
	10/9/18		3 Cases Admitted.	
	11/9/18		4 Cases Admitted.	
	12/9/18		1 Case Admitted. 4 Cases transferred. 3 Remount castings transferred.	
	13/9/18		2 Cases Admitted.	
	14/9/18		1 Case Admitted.	
	15/9/18		1 Case Admitted.	
	16/9/18		5 Cases Admitted. 8 cases transferred.	
	17/9/18		No. 33297 Pte Channings R, No. 34586 Pte Reed A. joined Section from No. 2 V.H. 1 Case Admitted.	
	18/9/18		No. 6519 A/Cpl Harris J.W. & No. 18208 Pte Holt J. dispatched to No 2 V.H. for further training for appt. of Sergt. Arc. to Field Units. 1 Case transferred.	32nd MOBILE VETERINARY SECTION 20th DIVISION

Army Form C. 2118.

Instructions regarding War Diaries and Intelligence Summaries are contained in F. S. Regs., Part II. and the Staff Manual respectively. Title pages will be prepared in manuscript.

WAR DIARY
or
INTELLIGENCE SUMMARY.
(*Erase heading not required.*)

September.

Place	Date	Hour	Summary of Events and Information	Remarks and references to Appendices
PETIT SERVINS	19/9/18		2 Cases Admitted. 2 Cases transferred.	
	20/9/18		3 Cases Admitted. 2 Cases transferred.	
	21/9/18		9 Cases Admitted. 1 Case Butchered.	
	22/9/18		No. 15285 Pte. Bocking CA returned from leave. 7 cases transferred.	
	23/9/18		5 Cases admitted.	
	24/9/18		9 Cases Admitted. 1 case Butchered.	
	25/9/18		T/31533 Dr. Brown A proceeded on 14 days leave to England. 6 cases Admitted. 10 case transferred, 1 Case Butchered.	
	26/9/18		No. 6455. Pte. Rose T admitted to 60th Field Ambulance. 3 cases Admitted. 6 cases transferred, 1 Case Butchered.	
	27/9/18		5 Cases Admitted.	
	28/9/18		4 Cases Admitted. 10 Cases transferred	
	29/9/18		1 Case Admitted.	
	30/9/18		7 Cases Admitted.	

P. Lindsay Capt. A.V.C.

22nd MOBILE VETERINARY SECTION, 20th DIVISION.
No.............
Date...........

A5834 Wt. W4973/M687 750,000 8/16 D. D. & L. Ltd. Forms/C.2118/13.

19

Instructions regarding War Diaries and Intelligence Summaries are contained in F. S. Regs., Part II. and the Staff Manual respectively. Title pages will be prepared in manuscript.

WAR DIARY
or
INTELLIGENCE SUMMARY.
(Erase heading not required.)

October.

32 Mob. Vety Sec

Army Form C. 2118.

20

Place	Date	Hour	Summary of Events and Information	Remarks and references to Appendices
PETIT SERVINS	1/10/18.		No. 03491 Pte Buckland G. proceeded on 14 days leave to England. 4 cases admitted 2 cases Entrained.	V81
"	2/10/18		6 cases admitted. 10 cases transferred.	
"	3/10/18		2 cases admitted. 5 cases transferred.	
"	4/10/18		9 cases admitted. 2 cases transferred.	
"	5/10/18		No. T/382782 Dr. Allin G.A. A.S.C. joined Section. 4 cases admitted. 9 transferred.	
MINGOVAL	6/10/18		Section marched to Mingoval. No. 6344 Pte Perry J.R. admitted to Hospital. 4 cases handed over to No. 18 M.V.S. at Petit Servins.	
"	7/10/18	—	Capt. Lindsay proceeded on leave to England. Major Lishman, D.A.D.V.S. acting. 2 cases admitted.	
"	8/10/18	—	1 case admitted	
"	10/10/18	—	1 " transferred	
"	11/10/18	—	2 " " , 1 case admitted	
12	12/10/18	—	1 " "	
"	13/10/18	—	No. T/31533 Dr Brown, A.S.C. returned from leave.	
"	15/10/18	—	2 cases admitted.	
"	16/10/18	—	1 case "	
"	17/10/18	—	1 " " , 1 case transferred.	

32nd MOBILE VETERINARY SECTION ... MV/20/41 1/11/18

A5834 Wt. W4973/M687 750,000 8/16 D. D. & L. Ltd. Forms/C.2118/13.

Instructions regarding War Diaries and Intelligence Summaries are contained in F. S. Regs., Part II. and the Staff Manual respectively. Title pages will be prepared in manuscript.

WAR DIARY
or
INTELLIGENCE SUMMARY.
(*Erase heading not required.*)

Army Form C. 2118.

October.

Place	Date	Hour	Summary of Events and Information	Remarks and references to Appendices
MINGOVAL.	18/10/18	—	No. 83882 Pte WATTS, F.W., returned to 20th Div. Salvage Coy. No. 30491 " BUCKLAND, G, A.V.C., returned from leave. 1 case admitted	
"	19/10/18	—	3 cases admitted, 2 cases transferred.	
"	20/10/18	—	No. T/3/027154 Dr HOPKINSON, T.H., A.S.C. proceeded on 14 days leave to England. 1 case cured.	
"	21/10/18	—	3 cases transferred.	
"	22/10/18	—	2 " admitted.	
"	23/10/18	—	Capt. Lindsay returned from leave. T. Lishman Maj. A.V.C. 23.10.18	
"	24/10/18		6 cases admitted. 1 destroyed.	
	25/10/18		No. 33296 Pte. Channings R. proceeded on 14 days leave to England. 3 cases admitted.	
	26/10/18		3 cases admitted. 10 cases transferred.	
	27/10/18		1 case admitted.	
	28/10/18		No. 7583 Pte. Bromley H. + No. 6727 Pte Knight A proceeded on 14 days leave to England. 4 cases admitted.	
	29/10/18		3 cases admitted.	
	30/10/18		1 case Butchered. 9 transferred	
	31/10/18		No. 9738 Pte Jarman E. proceeded on 14 days leave to England. Section [illegible] for veter.	

P. Lindsay. Capt. A.V.C.

92nd MOBILE VETERINARY SECTION
MV/20/41
31/10/18

A5834 Wt. W4973/M687 750,000 8/16 D. D. & L. Ltd. Forms/C.2118/13.

27

Instructions regarding War Diaries and Intelligence Summaries are contained in F. S. Regs., Part II. and the Staff Manual respectively. Title pages will be prepared in manuscript.

WAR DIARY
or
INTELLIGENCE SUMMARY.
(*Erase heading not required.*)

32 Mob Vety Sec

November. 1918

Army Form C. 2118.

20

Place	Date	Hour	Summary of Events and Information	Remarks and references to Appendices
VELU	1/11/18.		Section detrained Velu & marched to Cambrai. 1 case admitted.	
CAMBRAI	2/11/18.		2 Cases Admitted.	
	3/11/18.		Section Marched from Cambrai to Rieux. 3 cases admitted. 3 cases transferred.	
RIEUX.	4/11/18.		1 Case Admitted.	
	5/11/18		4 cases transferred.	
	6/11/18		Section marched from Rieux to Vendegies. 1 case admitted.	
VADEGIES	7/11/18		Nil.	
	8/11/18		Section Marched to Wargnies le Grand. 4 cases admitted.	
WARGNIES LE GRAND	9/11/18		Section Marched to Bavay. 1 case admitted	
BAVAY	10/11/18		1 case admitted. No. T/3/027154 Dr. Hopkinson T.H. returned from leave.	
	11/11/18		1 case admitted. 1 case destroyed.	
	12/11/18		4 cases Admitted.	
	13/11/18		7 cases Admitted. 10 cases transferred.	
	14/11/18		8 cases admitted.	
	15/11/18		16 cases ~~admitted~~ PTL. transferred. 8 cases admitted.	
	16/11/18		10 cases admitted.	
	17/11/18		1 Case admitted. 9 cases transferred.	
	18/11/18		6 Cases Admitted.	
	19/11/18		No. 7583 Pte Bromley H. " 6727 " Knight A. " 9738 " Jarman E. } returned from leave. 7 cases admitted. 9 cases transferred.	
	20/11/18		1 Case admitted.	

32ND MOBILE VETERINARY SECTION, 29TH DIVISION. No. .... Date ....

Instructions regarding War Diaries and Intelligence Summaries are contained in F. S. Regs., Part II. and the Staff Manual respectively. Title pages will be prepared in manuscript.

WAR DIARY
or
INTELLIGENCE SUMMARY.
(Erase heading not required.)

Army Form C. 2118.

November.

Place	Date	Hour	Summary of Events and Information	Remarks and references to Appendices
BAVAY	21/11/18		23 case admitted. 20 cases transferred	
	22/11/18		9 cases admitted. 10 cases transferred.	
	23/11/18		Section marched to Jenlain.	
JELAIN	24/11/18		1 case admitted.	
	25/11/18		Section marched to Vendigies. 1 case transferred No. 19756 Pte Stevenson A. proceeded on 14 days leave to England.	
VENDIGIES	26/11/18		Section marched to Rieux, 2 cases admitted. 1 case transferred.	
RIEUX	27/11/18		1 case admitted. 3 cases transferred	
	28/11/18		Section marched to Cambrai.	
CAMBRAI	29/11/18		Section marched to Beugnatre.	
BEUGNATRE	30/11/18		Section marched to Bienvillers.	

32ND MOBILE VETERINARY SECTION. 20TH DIVISION.
No. 7a/1/26/69
Date 1/12/18

P. Sheridan
Capt. AVC.

A5834 Wt. W4973/M687 750,000 8/16 D. D. & L. Ltd. Forms/C.2118/13.

14 20

Instructions regarding War Diaries and Intelligence Summaries are contained in F. S. Regs., Part II. and the Staff Manual respectively. Title pages will be prepared in manuscript.

WAR DIARY
or
INTELLIGENCE SUMMARY.
(Erase heading not required.)

Army Form C. 2118.

32 Mob Vety Sec

VIII 41

Place	Date	Hour	Summary of Events and Information	Remarks and references to Appendices
Bienvillers	1/12/18		Section marched to Pas.	
Pas.	3/12/18		6 cases admitted.	
"	4/12/18		3 do do. 8 cases transferred & 1 case butchered.	
"	5/12/18		Capt. P.T. Lindsay A.V.C. left Division to assume appointment of D.A.D.V.S. 55th Div. Major T Lishman D.A.D.V.S. 20th Div took over duties of 32nd M.V.S until arrival of another officer	32nd MOBILE VETERINARY SECTION, 20th DIVISION. No. ... Date ...
			1 Case admitted.	
	6/12/18		2 cases admitted.	
	7/12		1 Case transferred.	
"	8/12		1 case admitted 2 cases transferred. No1075 Cpl. Guy J & No 22225. Pte. Clarke. A. J. proceeded on 14 days leave to England	
	9/12		Capt. G K. Shaw A.V.C joined the Section from No 6. V.H	
			2 cases admitted, 1 case butchered.	
	10/12		3 cases transferred No 7459 Sgt. Mc Guinness. W. E. and No 9667 Cpl. Morgan K. proceeded on 14 days leave to England.	

A5834 Wt. W4973/M687 750,000 8/16 D. D. & L. Ltd. Forms/C.2118/13.

Army Form C. 2118.

Instructions regarding War Diaries and Intelligence Summaries are contained in F. S. Regs., Part II. and the Staff Manual respectively. Title pages will be prepared in manuscript.

WAR DIARY
or
INTELLIGENCE SUMMARY.
(Erase heading not required.)

Place	Date	Hour	Summary of Events and Information	Remarks and references to Appendices
Pas	11/12/18		No 15244 S.S. Day. W. proceeded on 14 days leave to Eng. 1 case admitted	
"	12/12/18		1 case destroyed.	
"	13/12/18		Routine.	
"	14/12/18		No 19756 Pte. Stevenson A. returned from leave. 4 cases admitted. 2 stray mules received from D 92 Bde R.F.A.	32nd MOBILE VETERINARY SECTION, 20th DIVISION. No. ...... Date ......
"	15/12/18		4 cases transferred.	
"	16/12/18		No 30491 Pte. Buckland G. returned to duty. 5 cases admitted.	
"	17/12/18		5 cases transferred.	
"	18/12/18		4 cases admitted.	
"	19/12/18		Routine as usual	
"	20/12/18		No 30491 Pte. Buckland G. despatched R.A.V.C. depot Woolwich. 4 cases admitted	
"			3 cases transferred 1 case destroyed.	
"	21/12/18		5 cases admitted. 3 cases transferred.	
"	22/		2 cases " . 7 cases transferred.	
"	23/		7 " " NO 6136. Sgt. Tatton G. admitted	
"	24/		8 " " 14 cases transferred. No 6136. Sgt. Tatton G. discharged from hospital.	
"	25/		Routine	
"	26/		"	
"	27/		"	
"	28/		No 15244 S.S Day W. Returned from leave. 13 cases admitted & transferred.	
"	29/		No 9667. Cpl Morgan K returned from leave.	
"	30		No 1033 Cpl Sny. J. & No 22225 Pte Clarke A J. returned from leave 1 case admitted	

S.K. Sloan Capt R.A.V.C

A5834. Wt. W4973/M687. 750,000 8/16 D. D. & L. Ltd. Forms/C.2118/13.

16

Instructions regarding War Diaries and Intelligence Summaries are contained in F. S. Regs., Part II. and the Staff Manual respectively. Title pages will be prepared in manuscript.

WAR DIARY
or
INTELLIGENCE SUMMARY.
(Erase heading not required.)

Army Form C. 2118.

20

32 Mob Vety Sec

January 1919

VR 4 R

Place	Date	Hour	Summary of Events and Information	Remarks and references to Appendices
PAS	1/1/19.		No 848 Pte. TIERNEY W proceeded on leave to UK for 14 days. 38 cases admitted to Section. 1 Mule (stray) admitted No 1079 Pte. Mc TIERNAN J. proceeded on 14 days leave to U.K. 19 cases transferred	
GRINCOURT	2/1/19		6 Cases admitted. 1 case destroyed. Section moved to GRINCOURT.	
	3/1/19		19 do do 22 cases transferred.	
	4/1/19		19 do do	
	5/1/19		No 07459 Sergt. Mc GUINNESS W.E. returned from leave. 10 cases admitted	
	6/1/19		14 Cases admitted 23 cases transferred.	
	7/1/19		Daily routine	
	8/1/19		No 0487 Sergt. WYBROW. V. No. 03456 Sergt FRAZER.T. 19370 Pte RADFORD. J 29145 Pte. LINTOTT. L. 16287 Pte. BROUGHTON. T. reported at Section for duty.	
	9/1/19		4 Cases admitted.	
	10/1/19		10 do do	
	11/1/19		Routine	
	12/1/19		10 cases admitted 2 cases transferred	
	13/1/19		22 cases transferred. 5 " admitted. Nos SE 6136 Sergt. TATTON. G. 7459 Sgt. Mc GUINNESS W.E. forward to LE HAVRE	

A5834 Wt. W4973/M687 750,000 8/16 D. D. & L. Ltd. Forms/C.2118/13.

Instructions regarding War Diaries and Intelligence Summaries are contained in F. S. Regs., Part II. and the Staff Manual respectively. Title pages will be prepared in manuscript.

WAR DIARY
or
INTELLIGENCE SUMMARY.
(Erase heading not required.)

January 1919.

Army Form C. 2118.

Place	Date	Hour	Summary of Events and Information	Remarks and references to Appendices
4/1/1 SRINCOURT	14/1/19		7 cases admitted.	
	15/1/19		2 do do. 1 case destroyed. 1 case transfered.	
	16/1/19		8 do do.	
	17/1/19		6 do do.	
	18/1/19		No 848 Pte. TIERNEY W. returned from leave.	
	19/1/19		Daily routine.	
	20/1/19		No 200846 A/Cpl. READ A.J. transferred to A.D.V.S. 17th Corps as clerk. 1 case admitted.	
	21/1/19		5 do do. 4 cases returned to their units. No 1079 Pte. McTIERNAN J. returned from leave.	
	22/1/19		24 cases transferred 1 case admitted.	
	23/1/19		3 cases admitted.	
	24/1/19		4 do do. 3 cases transferred. 1 Mule collected from Mde. Delbott Clairfaye Farm. belonging to 119th Inf. Bde. U.S. Army.	
	25/1/19		5 cases admitted.	
	26/1/19		2 do do.	
	27/1/19		12 cases transferred.	

D. D. & L., London, E.C.
(A5001) Wt. W1771/M2031 750,000 5/17 Sch. 52 Forms C2118/14

Army Form C. 2118.

Instructions regarding War Diaries and Intelligence Summaries are contained in F. S. Regs., Part II. and the Staff Manual respectively. Title pages will be prepared in manuscript.

WAR DIARY
or
INTELLIGENCE SUMMARY.
(Erase heading not required.)

January 1919

Place	Date	Hour	Summary of Events and Information	Remarks and references to Appendices
GRINCOURT	28/1/19		2 Cases admitted.	
	29/1/19		1 Case destroyed.	
	30/1/19		3 Cases admitted.	
	31/1/19		2 do do.	

G. K. Shaw Capt R.A.V.C
OC. 32nd M. V. Section

No. 32 MOBILE VETERINARY SECTION, 20TH DIVISION.
No. MV/20/168
Date. 1/2/19.

D. D. & L., London, E.C.
(A°001) Wt. W1771/M2031 750,000 5/17 Sch. 52 Forms C2118/14

Q

20th Div 17

Herewith War Diary for

Month of February 1919

S K [illegible] Capt

RAVC

O.C. 32nd M.V.S.

32nd MOBILE
VETERINARY SECTION
[illegible]

No. ......
Date 1/3/19

20

Army Form C. 2118.

Instructions regarding War Diaries and Intelligence Summaries are contained in F. S. Regs., Part II. and the Staff Manual respectively. Title pages will be prepared in manuscript.

WAR DIARY
or
INTELLIGENCE SUMMARY.
(Erase heading not required.)

32 Mob Vety Sec.

February. 1919.

VS 43

Place	Date	Hour	Summary of Events and Information	Remarks and references to Appendices
GRINCOURT	1st		General routine. D.A.D.V.S. visited Section. 1 case admitted	
	2nd		do do	
	3rd		do do 3 cases admitted.	
	4th		" " 4 " "	
	5th		" " 15 " transferred to 17th V.E.S.	
	6th		No 6727 Pte. KNIGHT A. proceeded to Corps Concentration camp for demobilization.	
	7th		2 cases transferred by float to 17th V.E.S.	
	8th		1 do admitted.	
	9th		5 do do	
	10th		1 do do 7 cases transferred to No 17 V.E.S.	
	11th		No 6317 Pte FINNEY W. reported at this Section for duty. 4 cases admitted	
	12th		1 case admitted.	
	13th		" "	
	14th		3 " " 9 cases transferred to 17th V.E.S	
	15th		1 "	
	16th		No 0487 Sergt. WYBROW. V. admitted to hospital	
	17th		1 case admitted. 50 animals admitted for sale at AVESNES LE COMTE	
	19th		3 cases admitted. 48 " sold at AVESNES LE COMTE 2 returned (Not sold.	
	20th		6 cases admitted	

D. D. & L., London, E.C.
(A7092) Wt. W1771/M2031 750,000 5/17 Sch. 52 Forms C2118/14

Army Form C. 2118.

WAR DIARY
or
INTELLIGENCE SUMMARY.
(Erase heading not required.)

Instructions regarding War Diaries and Intelligence Summaries are contained in F. S. Regs., Part II. and the Staff Manual respectively. Title pages will be prepared in manuscript.

February 1919.

Place	Date	Hour	Summary of Events and Information	Remarks and references to Appendices
GRINCOURT.	21st		8 cases transferred to 17th V.E.S. 1 case admitted	
	22nd		20 "D" cases arrived at Section for 1 night.	
	23rd		20 "D" cases left for ARRAS. 20 D. cases arrived for 1 night	
	24th		20 "D" cases left for ARRAS. 1 case transferred to 17th V.E.S	
			58 Surplus 2 animals admitted for sale.	
	26th		60 surplus 2 " sold at AVESNES LE COMTE	
	27th		8 cases admitted.	
	28th		8 " transferred to 17th V.E.S.	

S. K. Slaw Capt R.A.V.C.
O.C. 32nd M.V.S.
28/2/19

D. D. & L., London, E.C. (A5oo.) Wt. W1271/M2031 750,000 5/17 Sch. 52 Forms C2118/14

Instructions regarding War Diaries and Intelligence Summaries are contained in F. S. Regs., Part II. and the Staff Manual respectively. Title pages will be prepared in manuscript.

19

WAR DIARY
or
INTELLIGENCE SUMMARY.
(Erase heading not required.)

32 MVS

March Vol 1919. 34

Army Form C. 2118.

Place	Date	Hour	Summary of Events and Information	Remarks and references to Appendices
GRINCOURT	1st		A.D.V.S 17th Corps visited Section 4 cases admitted.	
	2nd		1 case admitted.	
	5th		6 do. Sold 91 class Z animals at AVESNES LES COMTE.	
	6th		D.A.D.V.S. visited Section	
	7th		1 case admitted. 18 class Z animals sold at PAS.	
	9th		2 do.	
	10th		11 cases transferred. D.A.D.V.S. visited Section	
	12th		2 " admitted. 64 class 2 animals sold at AVESNES LES COMTE	
	13th		1 " " D.A.D.V.S. visited Section	
	14th		2 " transferred	
	15th		Routine.	
	16th		D.A.D.V.S. visited Section	
	17th		Divisional General inspected Section. 3 cases admitted 91 'Z' animals admitted for Sale.	
	18th		Routine	
	19th		91 'Z' animals sold at AVESNES LES COMTE.	
	20th		Routine. D.A.D.V.S visited Section	
	21st		Nos. SE15244 S.S. Day. W; TT04482 Pte. Reed A; SE19370 Pte. Radford J; SE29105 Pte. Lintott L; SE6312 Pte. Finney W. transferred to 17. V.E.S. 5 cases transferred	

D. D. & L. London, E.C. (A"00) Wt. 1 71/M2031 750,000 5/17 Sch. 52 Forms C2..0/14

Instructions regarding War Diaries and Intelligence Summaries are contained in F. S. Regs., Part II. and the Staff Manual respectively. Title pages will be prepared in manuscript.

WAR DIARY
or
INTELLIGENCE SUMMARY.
(Erase heading not required)

Army Form C. 2118.

March. 1919.

Place	Date	Hour	Summary of Events and Information	Remarks and references to Appendices.
GRINCOURT	22nd		32nd M.V.S. reduced to Cadre and ceased to function as a Unit.	
	23rd		No's SE15788 Pte. Draking G.A. SE19756 Pte. Stevenson A.A; SE 25754 Pte. Smith C transferred to No 2 Vety. Hospital Le Havre.	
	24th		Checked and took stock of Stores.	
	25th		D.A.D.V.S. visited Section	
	26th		" " " Received orders to proceed to No 14 Vety. Hospital ABBEVILLE.	
	27th		Cadre of 32nd M.V.S. joined the Divisional Train.	
	28th		Capt. G.K. Shaw R.A.V.C. proceeded to No 14 Vety. Hospital.	

G.K. Shaw Capt. R.A.V.C.
O.C. 32nd M.V.S.

28/3/19.

D. D. & L., London, E.C. A(00) Wt. 1 71/M2031 750,000 5/17 Sch. 52 Forms C2.-0/14

www.ingramcontent.com/pod-product-compliance
Lightning Source LLC
Chambersburg PA
CBHW081544160426
43191CB00011B/1836